For The Sake of the Children

To Vera, who simply loved her grandchildren

For The Sake of the Children

THE FNF Guide to Shared Parenting

Sue Secker

FNF PUBLICATIONS

Copyright © Sue Secker & Families Need Fathers 2001
First published in 2001 by FNF Publications
Families Need Fathers
134 Curtain Road, London EC2A 3AR
e-mail: fnf@fnf.org.uk

Distributed by Gazelle Book Services Limited
Falcon House, Queen Square, Lancaster, England LA1 1RN

The right of Sue Secker to be identified as the author of the work has been asserted herein in accordance with the Copyright, Designs and Patents Act 1988.

Readers must assess the value of the information in this guide themselves. Neither FNF nor the author can accept any liability for any errors or omissions (also see p6).

Similarly, references herein to relevant law or legal procedures are intended to provide a general and basic outline. Any such information is not to be construed as advice to be relied upon, or acted upon, by any particular person(s) in relation to any specific circumstances

British Library Cataloguing in Publication Data
A catalogue record for this book is available from the British Library

ISBN 0-9539307-0-X

Typeset by Amolibros, Watchet, Somerset
This book production has been managed by Amolibros
Printed and bound by Professional Book Supplies, Oxford, England

Dedication

Your children are not your children
They are the sons and daughters of Life's longing for itself.
They come through you but not from you,
And though they are with you yet they belong not to you.
You may give them your love but not your thoughts,
For they have their own thoughts.
You may house their bodies but not their souls
For their souls dwell in the house of tomorrow,
Which you cannot visit, not even in your dreams.
You may strive to be like them, but seek not to make them like you.
For life goes not backward, nor tarries with yesterday.

(An extract from *The Prophet* by Kahlil Gibran)

ACKNOWLEDGEMENTS

Families Need Fathers would like to thank all who contributed to this project, especially the following:

The Home Office: The guide was made possible by a Family Support Grant from the Family Policy Unit of the Home Office. This valuable contribution to the charitable work of FNF is greatly appreciated.

Related Organisations: A range of organisations and charities that share similar concerns were contacted as part of the background research, including:

Gingerbread, Grandparents Federation, Mothers Apart from Their Children, National Council for One Parent Families, National Stepfamily Association (now part of Parentline Plus), National Association of Child Contact Centres, Childline, the Family Court Welfare Service.

Seminars: National Council for Family Proceedings and Family Policy Studies Centre seminars provided helpful insights into the views of professionals and academics working with families.

FNF members and their families made the most valuable contribution to this project. The guide would not have been possible without their generous responses to requests for information or advice.

Critical readers (members of FNF and others) volunteered to read various drafts of the guide. Their constructive comments undoubtedly shaped and improved the final version.

Research support: Dr Ian Buchanan, University College Northampton.
Main project managers: Jim Parton, Chairman of FNF and John Baker, School of Applied Social Sciences, University of Brighton.

The guide was researched and compiled for FNF by Sue Secker MA.

Special thanks to Dodie Masterman for her illustrations, and to Tony Denton (and friends) for the cover photograph.

Extract from The Prophet by Kahlil Gibran reproduced by kind permission of the Gibran National Committee, PO Box 116-52375, Beirut, Lebanon.

WHAT IS FAMILIES NEED FATHERS?

Founded in 1974, FNF is a registered charity dedicated to 'Keeping Children and Parents in Contact'. It is the main provider of both practical and emotional support for parents apart from children. FNF is reliant upon membership subscriptions and donations, yet each year meets the needs of thousands of parents who seek sympathetic, practical support during the confusing and stressful experience of divorce or separation. Some members remain active in FNF long after their own family problems have been resolved, providing encouragement and support to newer members.

Support is provided through a network of local contacts and branch meetings (all organised by volunteers). FNF also publishes a regular newsletter and a range of leaflets and booklets, and has a comprehensive website.

FNF promotes shared parenting and equality after divorce or separation. It campaigns to raise awareness of the consequences for children when they lose contact with one of their parents (usually, but not always the father). It supports the use of family mediation to reduce conflict and potential harm to the children. Until policies and practices concerned with family breakdown reinforce the right of children to benefit from the care and involvement of both parents, there will continue to be a need for FNF.

> "Men have always had problems discussing their feelings. A show of emotion is considered unmanly, yet there is not one father in FNF who has not secretly cried about the loss of his children. Putting those tears on paper would produce more results than all the lawyers in the kingdom."
>
> (Stan Haywood 1999)

This guide draws on the experiences of FNF members past and present in order *to help parents make their own positive and realistic decisions about their family situation.* Wherever possible original contributions and quotations have been included, but personal details have been changed to protect the identities of families.

The advice offered is practical rather than idealistic: families have to face the world as it is now, not as it could be. It will be of interest to anyone who wants to reduce conflict and increase support for children when parents live apart.

PREFACE BY PAUL BOATENG

The Rt Hon Paul Boateng MP
Deputy Home Secretary

Children with two involved parents are happier, healthier, do better at school, are less likely to get into trouble, and go on to have better and more stable relationships and families. Best of all is where two loving and caring parents live happily together. However, this is not always possible, and the benefits of shared parenting still apply where parents live apart. The distress and damage done to children when parents separate can be reduced if they retain strong loving bonds with both parents. Sharing responsibility for children is also good for parents. Both can enjoy the emotional rewards of caring for them. Both can earn for their family and lead more balanced lives.

As a constituency MP, I have seen how families can suffer when parents split up. As a government minister concerned with both supporting families and preventing crime, I want to make sure all children are given the best opportunities for a good start in life.

Parents want what is best for their children. They often find it hard to access good advice and support, especially about what to do for their children when they and their ex-partner do not live together. They may make inappropriate and sometimes short-term decisions. They may get angry and distressed and that is bound to affect not only themselves but their children and those around them. That is why the government is committed to supporting families through divorce, to ensure minimal impact upon children.

We are working to create an environment that allows all families to flourish, by supporting parents and ensuring all children have the opportunity to succeed. One way in which we do this is through the Family Support Grant, where we are working with voluntary organisations both to increase the support available to parents and to raise public awareness of the importance of parenting by enabling a range of voices to add to the parenting debate.

The mission of Families Need Fathers is to help children by helping their parents to stay involved with the family after divorce or separation. I am delighted that the

Home Office, through the Family Support Grant, was able to fund this guide to provide practical help and support for parents trying to support their children through a difficult and often bewildering experience.

Paul Boateng

Although this publication has been funded by the Home Office, it has been prepared by Families Need Fathers and the views expressed in this document are not necessarily those of the government.

CONTENTS

Introduction

THE NEED FOR INFORMATION, ADVICE, SUPPORT

Being apart from dearly loved children is indescribably painful, for mothers *and* fathers. It is also deeply upsetting for other relations, grandparents, uncles, aunts, etc., who have known and loved the children. Separation from a loved and loving family is distressing and damaging for children.

The sense of loss can be overwhelming. Men may find it difficult to show they are suffering emotionally. Nevertheless, they are just as hurt, and in need of support.

Parents (mainly fathers) contact FNF because they want to continue to play a meaningful part in their children's upbringing. Many will be having difficulty negotiating contact arrangements either with the other parent or via a court agreement. Some will have little or no contact at all, despite being willing and able to be more involved.

Grandparents and members of the wider family contact FNF for the same reason. They also suffer the consequences of less or lost contact with children who once were part of their lives. It is difficult for them to imagine why children should not continue to benefit from these special family relationships. Many new partners also seek advice because they recognise the distress to their partners and children and don't know how best to help.

An added pressure is that those caught in this situation may have difficulty discussing these issues in case it makes matters worse for their family. If they are in the middle of court proceedings, they are legally bound not to disclose certain information that might identify children. Anything that could be judged negatively is likely to influence the court's decision.

It is difficult to remain calm and focused when the whole process is unintelligible, seems to drag on for ages, with the risk that the slightest show of emotion might be misjudged and count against you.

> **Finding that the relationship you once had with your children is slipping away**
>
> **That there appears to be little you can do to stop it happening**
>
> **No service to whom you can turn for support and advice**
>
> **No one who is able to prevent this happening**
>
> **IS AN ISOLATING AND DEEPLY STRESSFUL EXPERIENCE.**

There is little empathy with parents, usually fathers, who find this happening to their family. They are mainly seen as unable to come to terms with a situation judged as inevitable. They need advice, information and guidance on how best to cope with the frustration and powerlessness. They especially need sympathetic support. Some can find all this and more at FNF local branch meetings. Discovering that others are 'in the same boat' can be a lifeline. There are many reasons why it may not be possible to get to a meeting. Those that cannot, or choose not to, do this may still need that lifeline.

Don't give up hope

This guide is based on the firsthand experiences of many members of FNF and their families, past and present. The one clear message that comes across is: '***Don't give up hope.***' Everyone who understands the ache of separation from children either firsthand or having watched someone close to them suffering has said the same thing.

Things may improve: eventually children who once thought Dad (or Mum) didn't care or worse, had abandoned them, might begin to realise they were loved after all. It happens all the time. Hopefully this will strengthen your own natural desire to be involved with your children, and encourage you not to give up on this even when it becomes difficult.

> ➤ *You are right to want to be there for them.*
> ➤ *Don't feel guilty.*
> ➤ *Don't let anyone persuade you that you are wrong.*
> ➤ *It is absolutely natural to love your children.*
> ➤ *It is their right to know that you do.*

That's the easy bit: dealing with all the complex and stressful surrounding issues is not so easy.

> *No one knows what lies ahead when their*
> *family splits up. You will need all the help*
> *available to make sense of what is happening*
> *as soon as possible. Mistakes made early on*
> *may set the pattern for all that is to follow,*
> *and if not managed positively can seriously*
> *affect the prospects for a continuing*
> *relationship with children.*

It is often only looking back that we recognise where things went wrong, the mistakes we made with good intentions at the time. This could be due to lack of information, not understanding 'the system' and also to making assumptions about what should or could happen next.

Parts One and Two of this guide offer practical advice on how best to cope positively with the many changes and situations that you may have to face.

Part Three includes a brief overview of the law relating to families, and the people who might become involved as you try to sort out the next part of your parenting life.

Part Four is a reference section and includes other sources of information, and suggestions for further reading.

The ultimate aim in the short- and long-term, is to help you maintain the best relationship possible with your children, whatever the circumstances.

Limitations of the guide

➢ The guide is not a panacea: you will not find magic answers or quick-fix solutions.

➢ It cannot change reality: you must deal with what has to be faced now.

➢ It cannot change attitudes overnight.

➢ It cannot offer a blueprint for any specific family situation, or individual: the vast differences between families and individuals make this impossible.

A word of caution about taking advice

Advice from professionals you may meet, or even other FNF members, is often phrased so authoritatively, that it appears as if it is the only course of action open. It can be very persuasive, but there may well be other alternatives, ones perhaps more suitable for you and your family. Bear in mind that this advice may be based on opinions, albeit opinions born out of professional or personal experience. Some members of FNF have special expertise and considerable experience: others may best offer support and sympathy. Always seek more than one opinion, preferably a wide range, then make a decision based on what suits you and your family situation. If you feel uncomfortable with whatever is suggested, it may not be right for you. Only you can weigh up the personalities involved, how people might react.

☛   *Always consider the impact upon your children*   ☛

Basic principles

Although there can never be a solution or plan of action that suits every individual or set of circumstances, there does appear to be a consensus about the best way to proceed if you are able to do so.

> ➤   Children should be free to receive the maximum support from the widest possible family network, especially when the relationship between their parents has broken down.

> ➤   Both parents should encourage this support.

> ➤   Do try to work out informal agreements regarding arrangements for children with the other parent.

> ➤   Don't assume you will not be able to do this.

> ➤   Do take action quickly if all attempts to reach agreement fail, and your children are losing contact with you.

> ➤   Don't assume it is in their interests to 'give up' for whatever reason.

The guide is therefore based on these simple child-centred principles. In many respects, it will suggest how you can make the best of situations that should not exist in the first place. *You are not on your own.* FNF has a long history of supporting families as they try to make sense of life after divorce or relationship breakdown. Most sort out their problems eventually. *Don't ever give up hope.*

SETTING THE SCENE

It is estimated that at least one in four children will have experienced the breakdown of their parents' relationship by the time they reach sixteen. The average length of a relationship before it falters is around seven years; therefore most children will be very young when their parents part. The majority will subsequently live with one parent (almost always the mother) for a while.

Children are vulnerable at such times, and any arrangement for their lives must be sensitive to their needs. Some families will be able to sort out such arrangements amicably. At the other end of the spectrum, many seek court orders because they are unable to resolve problems. The number of parents applying for court orders for children is rising steadily. These applications are not only made at the time of separation but also when problems arise, sometimes years afterwards.

This may be the tip of the iceberg: thousands of families contact FNF every year. There must be others needing help who may not realise that they could get specialist advice, etc. from experienced organisations such as FNF. Men often feel they should be able to cope on their own. They may be afraid to ask, not know whom to ask. Many will not have considered they might ever need help, until they realise they

may be about to lose contact with their children.

This middle ground also includes those who have not really resolved the breakdown of their family in the best way possible for children. Some are simply too hurt, or have just accepted they cannot see their children. They may have decided the legal route is not for them. They may not be able to afford the legal costs, or not want to involve their children in a 'battle'.

The percentage of fathers who lose contact with children is quoted, but it is seldom acknowledged that this may not be their choice. The fathers who join FNF are not part of these 'lost father statistics'. They are often parents living apart from children, who in many cases did not have any say in the breakdown of their family, who undoubtedly want to continue to be responsible parents. They cannot understand why their input is not properly recognised. They miss being involved, part of their children's lives.

They speak of no longer being able to help with everyday things like reading bedtime stories, playing football at the park, or with homework. They may not have any input into major decisions like choice of schools, etc. Frankly, they miss just 'being there' for their children.

The other parent may be resisting their involvement, perhaps not co-operating over arrangements, or may have refused to allow any contact at all. That they are able to do this reflects the greater power they have to make decisions for children. Mums or dads living apart from children can experience the same exclusion, and be relatively powerless.

FNF has played a major role in raising awareness of the valuable contribution that each parent can and should make especially after family breakdown. Attitudes are beginning to change, and there is increasing recognition of the benefits to children when both parents can be involved in their upbringing.

Unmarried fathers and 'Parental Responsibility'

At present, unmarried fathers have no legal rights whatsoever in relation to their children unless they have made a legally binding agreement with the mother or obtained a court order. Having their name on the child's birth certificate or paying child support gives them no legal rights.

The Children Act 1989 introduced the concept of Parental Responsibility (PR). All mothers and all married fathers automatically have PR for their children, but an unmarried father does not (Court Orders concerning children p72).

The significance of PR is often not appreciated until it is too late, when the relationship between parents has broken down and decisions about children need to be made. If the father does not have PR, only the mother has the right to make *any* decisions concerning children, from giving consent for an emergency operation, to whether they can be taken abroad on holiday. The father has no legal role, even if the children are put up for adoption. The father can, however, make application to the court in relation to these and other matters (either with or without leave of the court).

Services dealing with adoption have a duty to make reasonable enquiries about *both birth parents* when they are preparing their report for the court. Unmarried fathers without PR should be given the opportunity to express their wishes. The court should take these into account if they have had a relationship with their children at any time. There is insufficient time and limited funding available for extensive searches. Inevitably, some fathers may not be 'found', and others learn of the imminent adoption too late to make any difference to the decision. (Also see Holidays overseas p33 and Change of name p52.)

Unmarried fathers can acquire Parental Responsibility for their children by making a Parental Responsibility Agreement with the mother on a standard form (one for each child). Both parents must sign the form in the presence of an authorised official and lodge the agreement at the Principal Registry of the Family Division. There is no fee. Informal agreements i.e. not on form C(PRA) and not registered as above, have no legal status.

If the mother will not agree, the father can apply to court for a Parental Responsibility Order (PRO). The court will want to see some evidence of prior involvement or commitment to the child. Few fathers are refused PR by the courts. An appeal against a refusal is usually successful. FNF produces an information sheet with detailed advice about drawing up an agreement, and making a successful application for PR. This information is also on the FNF website.

Always bear in mind that the reaction to legal action may be increased hostility (so timing may be crucial), but it is essential for your continuing involvement in your children's lives that you acquire PR. In many cases, the mother will agree before the case gets to court.

Mediation/conciliation

"Mediation helps couples to turn an argument into a negotiation."
(Thelma Fisher, National Family Mediation, 1997)

> *A contested court case is something that all parents*
> *should avoid if at all possible.*

It is important for separating parents to consider using mediation to reduce any potential for conflict for children. Unresolved conflict can affect relationships for years. If there is any residual goodwill between parents, mediation provides a real opportunity to reduce problems for the children. The service is not free, but successful use of mediation is likely to save money.

Note: The aim of mediation or conciliation is not to get you back together with the other parent. (**Re-conciliation** is undertaken by other agencies e.g. Relate.)

Mediation is a means of helping separating couples to make their own arrangements for the future with the help of an impartial third party. The main aim is to reduce unnecessary conflict by helping you and your family to get a better grasp of the issues that will have to be dealt with. You will be encouraged to explore common ground in the hope that you can reach an agreement. Where this is successful then a 'Parenting Plan' – a document agreed by the parents – may be suggested. This is likely to include a statement that the parents will work together in the children's interests, giving details of arrangements for holidays, schooling, medical treatment and other areas of potential dispute. There is an example on p106 in Thelma Fisher's book (details in Part Four of this book: No 47).

Many parents who try this process reach agreement. Even if you cannot agree, you might still reach some common ground. It also shows you are willing to co-operate. Remember that the court will want to see evidence that both parents have done all they can to try to resolve matters themselves. It is worth mentioning that all is usually confidential, and cannot be used to support any claims in court.

Mediation services can be run by a variety of agencies, including solicitors. The service provided rests largely with the individuals running your session/s. They come from different backgrounds, ranging from psychoanalysts to lawyers. Views and practices can vary widely. If you are uncertain or don't understand something, ask for more information. It makes sense to go with an open mind. If all co-operate there is a real opportunity to work through contentious issues, mindful of the impact upon your children. Don't be afraid or embarrassed to give this a try. It may reduce the problems for your children, which is after all the main concern.

Experience suggests that 'out of court' mediation is preferable to 'in court' services. The Family Court Welfare Service (FCWS: p80) may offer a conciliation service, aimed at trying to get an agreement between parents before the final court hearing. There is always a danger that you (and the other parent) may be rail-roaded into doing a deal. Don't let yourself be brow-beaten into something that you feel will not work, or is much less than your children need.

If you have applied for a court order perhaps because your children are not able to see you or your family, then subsequently you appear to have come to an agreement with the other parent, the court is unlikely to make an order. Only court orders have any legal standing. You may find that once the hearing is over, there is nothing to deter further resistance. This could mean yet another costly and stressful return to court, not to mention more disruption to your children's relationship with you. Be prepared to make a statement outlining your concerns, giving reasons why what's proposed might not ultimately be in their interests.

When there is disagreement about the way forward, how can conflict be reduced, and what could make it easier for children to benefit from the support of both parents?

Start from shared parenting principles

Decisions made early on, or the assumptions upon which these decisions are based, may set the pattern for much that is to come. For example, it is widely assumed that children will remain with mother. It is fair to say that mothers also presume that this will happen. They seldom question this outcome: *neither do fathers*.

"She has all the rights to the children."

Don't assume you must just accept a minor role in their lives. If you have PR (p8) you both have an equal right to take responsibility for your children when they are with you. And if you do not have PR, you will probably be able to obtain it. Even fathers without PR can sometimes make application to the court in order to protect the interests of the child or resolve an issue concerning that child.

The rise in applications for court orders concerning children has been put down to fathers now 'exercising their newly found rights'. There may be an element of truth in that, because information is becoming more readily available. However, it may really be more to do with fathers beginning to question the presumption that children are 'best left' with mother. They may apply for an order when they discover they are being excluded from their children's lives. Other legislation may actually be encouraging this exclusion (Child Support Act p59, p71). Children should be able to benefit from the best of both parents' worlds.

In reality, either parent can raise children. The debate about which parent is a better carer is largely irrelevant, especially when considering the long-term benefits of having a relationship with both parents. Each parent has their own qualities, strengths and weaknesses and children need them both, warts and all (Caring for children p41). So, the advice must be, when deciding on arrangements for children, try to work towards a plan that will involve sharing the care and upbringing, rather than assuming one parent will 'get' the children, the other be relegated to the second parenting division. If the other parent seems reluctant to consider this, focus on the advantages for everyone if care is shared.

How you share the care will depend on your circumstances. It doesn't mean them spending exactly half their time with each parent. The main thing is that they can still be part of each parent's life, and are encouraged to be so. *This does rely on both parents recognising that this is important for children.* Some children move freely between parents living in different countries. Others are not able or allowed to visit parents and wider family living just around the corner.

An uneven playing field

"The parent apart, but particularly a father, he must understand the playing field is not level and he is at the bottom of the field."

Many would say that current legislation (Children Act 1989 p72) laid out a level parenting playing field. It is how the game has since evolved that places one parent at a disadvantage. The following is from the Children Act 1989 Guidance and Regulations:

"A shared care order has the advantage of being more realistic in those cases where the child is to spend considerable amounts of time with both parents...and removes any impression that one parent is good and responsible whereas the other parent is not."

Regrettably, the same guidelines introduced the concept that a Shared Residence Order (p72) should seldom be granted. *"It is not expected that it will become a common form of order."* These orders are usually only thought workable when parents are able to co-operate. However, they may be more appropriate when one parent will not encourage the involvement of the other parent, because the child's right to have the support of both parents would then be reinforced and protected.

The precedent set if only one parent is treated as important may be difficult to reverse. Family services and professionals are inclined to work with the 'resident' parent and may even dismiss the relevance of the one that lives elsewhere. You will find that it is not only the other parent, but also other professionals who become involved, that will need persuading re the benefits of sharing care more equally. You may have to challenge what they consider 'reasonable contact', a vague and undefined phrase that can lead to confusion and conflict. Also, the conditions imposed may be unnatural and unworkable. It is up to you to argue for a better outcome, for the sake of your children. Try to set a workable pattern immediately you and the other parent part (Accommodation p30). Whatever routine develops can soon become the 'status quo'. Even if this means you are not seeing the children at all, the system is reluctant to disturb what is regarded as a working arrangement. Recent research shows this may not be taking children's wishes or needs fully into account.

> "You are doing the right thing: shared care is not unusual – it can and does work. PS. Thanks for the notification of the AGM. I shall not be able to attend because it is my week to look after the children."

Don't be put off by advice that it is more 'normal' for the children to live with one parent. It is far more normal to live with, or at least be able to be loved and supported by a much wider network of people. But it is not all doom and gloom – some judges will grant shared residence if they can be persuaded that it is an appropriate order in a particular case. *If you don't ask for it, you won't get it, but remember to carefully prepare your argument.*

Realistically, given current attitudes, you may not achieve as much involvement as your children should have. How then, can you best help them, especially if they live somewhere else? If you desperately want to be a parent after family breakdown, but are forced to play a minor role, or have no input at all, you will not need to be told you should 'get involved'. *It is more a question of how **can** you get involved.* You may have relatively little or no choice about when, where or even if you see your children.

The next section deals with the whole question of how to manage life as a parent in these frustrating and difficult circumstances. The first part focuses on how everything impacts upon children. At the end of the day, if you cannot change how the other parent or the courts have organised your role, they are stuck with the consequences too. There may be little you can do to change attitudes or behaviour. You and your children will therefore have to make the best of what you have.

PART ONE: Being Positive

WHAT *IS* BEST FOR CHILDREN?

Bringing up children is a demanding but rewarding job, and is often even more difficult after family breakdown. As all are making decisions for *your* family, the most repeated phrase you will hear is: *'Ah, but we have to consider the best interests of the child.'* All will think they know what's best. All too often, children will not be asked for *their* views, but, wherever possible, they should be included in decisions that affect them. In fact, there *is* no one answer, but the guiding principle must be that it is best for them if they continue to benefit from their relationship with both parents and wider family support network.

What would they choose?

Undoubtedly, children, if free to choose, want both their parents, preferably back together again. If this is not possible, then the best compromise is to be able to be loved and cared for by both, parenting business as usual if from separate bases. They do not want to be asked to choose between parents, and they should not be given the ultimate responsibility for decisions about their lives, especially if their expectations cannot in reality be met. They inevitably love both their parents, regardless. The distress that children of all ages may suffer, as they become aware that their parents no longer want to stay together is well documented.

> "I used to tell lies a lot, to try and make people believe I was leading a happy life."

The need to be included

A recent study of what children wanted in terms of support services at such times showed that they may feel isolated from events and decisions that will deeply affect their futures. They wanted to know what was happening, to be able to get information easily and informally. *The crucial thing to remember is that they should not be left out.* When parents are preoccupied with their own problems, coping with all the emotional turmoil, it is so easy to overlook the fact that children need help too, and it may be hard for them to find out what help is appropriate.

Even though their parents have decided not to live together, children need to know that the decision is based on the failure of that relationship, and is not because of them. When their lives are unsettled, they need extra reassurance that they are still loved by both parents. They can also feel that they are somehow responsible for what is happening: *'What did I do to make Dad (or Mum) leave?'* Make sure they don't blame themselves as they commonly will. It is also damaging if they mistakenly think that one parent is leaving *them* or that he or she is solely responsible for the break-up of the family.

Children can feel largely powerless as parents and other adults re-shape their futures, as is obvious from this child's comments:

> "It was very stressful: you can't do it right. Everything was dictated – I had no choice. I couldn't say anything to anyone because I was afraid it would make it worse."

If they feel they are being considered, whatever has to happen next, there is a greater chance of coping with the inevitable compromises that will have to follow for everyone. ('Why Are My Parents Separating?' is a story tape and booklet that parents might find useful to involve and support young children as their family changes. See Part Four: No 51.)

Conflicts of interest

As said earlier, there are many views about what's best for children, and many areas where there is disagreement even amongst 'experts'. The other thing that is not fully appreciated is that 'family life' after parents move apart is so very different to how it was before, when there was 'one base'. The same values and ideas about what is best for children cannot apply, need to be re-worked to take account of the restructure.

Despite different assumptions about what children need, there is both evidence and agreement that children suffer from the effects of conflict. All agree that conflict needs to be minimised. Separating one family unit into two is inevitably stressful. Not only are the financial problems immense, but there may also be resentment and/or an unwillingness to co-operate. As lives diverge, take on new identities, there may be even more conflicts of interests (New partners p62, Maintenance p56).

It is perhaps negative to assume that change in itself is the cause of problems, or that children cannot deal with change, must be protected from it. It is the way such changes are managed, how they are helped to cope with changes that is the crucial factor in how well they adapt. *Children are more flexible than is generally realised,* and can survive best, if a constructive example is set for them. Even when there are major areas of disagreement between parents, respect for the other's part in their life is essential if they are not to suffer deep, often long-term emotional damage.

Adapting to changes

For many children, the attempt to maintain a relationship with both parents after family breakdown is fraught with conflict. Many feel pressured to 'choose' between their parents, and suffer guilt because they may have to do so. One researcher described how children attempt to 'pare down their families' in order to cope with the competing demands. It is tragic for everyone, but especially the children, if they are effectively forced to reject part of their family.

Children learn to conform to the rules and cultural system in their original family. When there are two homes, there may be two sets of rules. Yet parents with international marriages report that children find it surprisingly easy to become bilingual and bicultural: *'Two homes are a cinch!'* It can have advantages, helping to broaden their understanding, making them more able to adapt. But, when conflict exists, when one home criticises the other, they may be interrogated, expected to pass on information, and this does cause problems.

> "I used to hate going home. I knew when I got there they would ask me all about what they've got, what washing machine, what's in the house, how may bedrooms, how much did the house cost, etc. As I got home, I used to quickly go upstairs to my room to escape it."

Children develop ways to cope with these conflicts. They become defensive, uncommunicative, afraid in fact to say anything lest they get one or the other parent into trouble. They develop *'watertight compartments in their minds'*. There is a grave risk that their values will be distorted and damaged by parents who cannot appreciate that such behaviour is influencing their future.

> "I had to lie to my mum. She used to talk my dad down all the time. I find it hard to trust women."

> "Don't quiz or interrogate your child about their other parent. Learn to mind your own business!"

19

Even if parents can manage to reduce their own conflict in order to shield their children, there still may be insecurity and fear of what the future holds. When parents are unable to manage the situation reasonably, for whatever reason, children are at greater risk.

Children still need both parents

The key factor is accepting their need of a continuing relationship with all those they knew and loved before the break-up of their parents' relationship. All should encourage them to benefit from this network of support. Security and stability is not simply having one home to live in; it is a state of mind.

"They need to know you both still love them unconditionally, despite your own problems."

Managing family changes in a child-centred manner is not easy. It may take many years to come to terms with the breakdown of the relationship. Both parents can feel insecure, hurt and angry, and especially fear 'losing' their children. As each attempts to do what they consider to be best, they may not realise how confusing it can be for children. Being the centre of so much love and attention can become an overwhelming responsibility.

"Make them secure. Tell them you'll always be there for them."

Awareness of possible problems for children is one thing: being able to do anything to prevent the damage is quite another. If your children live mainly elsewhere, how do you manage?

MAKING THE BEST OF BEING THE 'OTHER' PARENT

As with most things, a positive attitude can make a difference. If you are negative, if you fear rejection or failure, or if you don't recognise and deal firmly with behaviour that may harm your relationship with your children, they will lose out.

If you can remain focused on what your child needs from you in the short- and long-term, if you are determined to make the best of whatever opportunities there are to contribute to their lives, if you refuse to give up, your children will benefit.

Your attitude rubs off on them: their behaviour is affected by yours. You and they may not realise this at the time, especially if conflicts arise or if you see little of one another, but eventually, they will make sense of it all, look back and realise how much you cared, how hard you tried.

Be positive about your 'ex'-partner

(Through gritted teeth if need be!)

Your relationship with the other parent is going to be the biggest single thing that affects all your lives until your children become independent.

The breakdown of a once loving relationship does result in changed attitudes. However, one parent cannot simply be cast off, considered to be less important – imagine the gap in children's lives. FNF fathers who have not seen their child for months worry that the child will forget them. Children do not forget their dads: they think about them all the time, and it's amazing how the father/child relationship picks up where it left off.

> "A father went off to war, returning many months later. His young son ran towards him and jumped into his arms."

The key influence is the attitude of the other parent. They will give out either positive or negative signals. Children soon sense when all is 'OK', and they will react accordingly. If they sense that one parent disapproves of the other, they face difficult choices.

> "All the photos of their dad were taken out of the album. They were told not to say his name."

Children need a positive image of both their parents. Many parents die when their children are young; children can and do manage without them. The difference is that the surviving parent will want to keep a positive memory alive. The extended family also rallies round rather than taking 'sides'. So often when families break down, this is often the opposite of what happens. Even when arrangements and relationships begin on a reasonable footing, an event, a move, a change of whatever kind can suddenly put this in jeopardy. Some people unfortunately have to face animosity from the start. Sometimes it is a one-sided battle, one parent having no choice but to face the flack. Whichever situation you find yourself in, no matter what you have to deal with, positive thought and action creates more opportunities. How you conduct yourself also makes a difference. There are occasions when your behaviour may be misjudged (Walking on eggshells p26).

The parents who have fed their experiences into this book understand how difficult it can be to negotiate with the other parent. The next section is based on their positive suggestions, plus thoughts on what to avoid.

CONSIDERATION, CO-OPERATION, COMPROMISE, COMMUNICATION

Be considerate and listen

If you don't listen to each other, you have virtually no chance of reaching agreement. How will you work out what the problem is? It must be said that either parent can become confrontational. Ultimately, without a real desire to listen to each other, to take on board the issues that each finds important, you will not move forward. If the other parent chooses not to listen, it's still best to choose the less adversarial route, unless of course, the child is at risk, for example if they are not free to continue their relationship with the rest of their family. If this happens, you must find ways to help them.

Co-operate

Try to be flexible even if it means making compromises. Everything can become competitive, no one prepared to back down lest this shows weakness, especially if that weakness might then be exploited by the 'other side'. Focus on the effect all this uncertainty will have upon children. The example set, the way those they are closest to resolve the problems, will undoubtedly have an influence upon their future behaviour. For their sakes, try to show you are prepared to try to work with the other parent.

Compromise

It's impossible miraculously to make a contentious situation perfect for all. Compromises are needed all round. They are easier to accept if everyone understands what's happening, and if it is accepted that all are making a positive effort to reach agreement. Focus on long-term aims and be prepared to give way sometimes in order to achieve these. Don't expect things to be sorted out quickly. It can be a slow process, gradually improving arrangements, clearing up misconceptions and building trust (between all concerned, including others that may become involved).

Open up channels of communication

If you cannot talk to one another, there is a real danger that attitudes will harden and decisions will be based on assumptions, not facts. Try not to jump to conclusions or immediately think the worst. It is so easy to project your own anxiety, disapproval and insecurity upon your children, especially when you are still suffering from the separation and perhaps feel let down. Unresolved emotional turmoil causes all kinds of over-reactions, including stopping children's contact with their other parent. The parent having problems re-adjusting needs help to focus on how this is harmful for the children. Try to empathise with the other parent – they will also be feeling insecure. It takes time to adjust: *both of you will have to adapt to being apart from children.* Watching you 'take them away' may not be easy.

> "Look out for opportunities to have calm discussions with the ex. They are not angry all the time!"

Even if you think it will be pointless, don't be afraid to make contact with your ex-partner or his or her family. There is no way you can predict the reaction, so don't make assumptions: you may get it very wrong. Perhaps a friend of each partner meeting, or a neutral third party can get some of the main misapprehensions out of the way, get dialogue re-started. A good place to aim for is recognition by both parties that each loves the children. Then, moving on from there, that the children love each parent. There is less justification for denying this loving relationship if these basic things can be defined.

Give the benefit of the doubt

If there is little or no communication, you might not have enough information to judge what's really happening.

"She did this deliberately. She knows this is my weekend. Why couldn't she have at least phoned me?"

When arrangements to collect children are disrupted, it is not easy to cope with the frustration and disappointment, especially if you have travelled hundreds of miles to be with them as some parents do. Try not to misjudge the motives of the other parent until you have had an opportunity to find out what went wrong.

If the disruption becomes a regular pattern or if the other parent refuses to discuss the situation, you must decide what you can do to improve things, especially for children. Don't back off, or just go away. If they are in the middle of this kind of situation, especially if they are young, they will be unable to judge what's happening. It will not help if you just disappear. They might end up thinking you abandoned them, didn't care. It may take many years for them to readjust their understanding of events.

Drawing the line

All the above advice about being flexible, trying to accommodate the needs of others is a good example for children too. However, sometimes you just have to say 'enough is enough'. You may be expected to agree to arrangements, etc. that you cannot realistically meet. Perhaps you will be asked to collect children at times that are really inconvenient, e.g. are incompatible with your working pattern. The other parent may push you to your limit. If you eventually decide to make it clear that you have done all you can, but are not prepared to give in yet again, they may realise they must change course. Be warned this can lead to threats of reprisals (usually about less or no contact) unless demands are met. In FNF's experience, a high proportion of contact disputes are really about money even though they are separate areas of law.

A common time for such threats is after holiday arrangements have been agreed. Suddenly children will not be able to go with you unless certain conditions are met, e.g. *'Pay for this now, or they can't come.'* Children who had been looking forward to the holiday will be disappointed and uncertain. What should you do? If you decide that you must take some action to prevent further harm being done, consider carefully before issuing ultimatums. You are best placed to know the personality and possible reaction of the other parent. You must be prepared to take the consequences if things get worse. It is not easy to 'make waves', even when the reason for standing ground is really important. Weigh up how the children will be affected, depending on which course you choose. Remember they may get confusing signals about what is acceptable behaviour, be equally damaged if they watch one parent manipulate the other.

"They've been divorced for years but the whole of my life my dad has had to do what she wants him to do. It's a power struggle. He's such a push over."

Reasonable behaviour may be perceived as weak: behaving unreasonably may be seen as getting results. Understandably, it can be difficult to find a 'right time' to discuss sensitive issues, especially if the time spent with children is limited. On the other hand, appeasing the other parent (or children) no matter how they behave, may simply be storing up problems for the future.

Admitting you make mistakes, but you still love your children

If you are responsible for the end of the relationship, for example if it was you who found another partner, it is inevitable that the parent 'left behind' will feel angry and resentful. The children may also feel betrayed or abandoned, and if the adults around them are less than tactful (be fair, it will be difficult for them not to be partisan), these feelings will be reinforced.

In these circumstances, they may stop you seeing the children for a time. They may tell you that the children do not want to see you. This doesn't mean they do not love you. They may not fully understand what's happening. They need reassurance, to know that despite the relationship between their parents ending, you still love them and need them. Keep up some form of indirect contact with them during this difficult time. Don't assume they won't open your letters. Just seeing a letter arrive on the doormat is a start, even if they aren't allowed to read it.

One father advised getting all this out in the open, admitting you acted badly, asking your family to try to understand what happened and to forgive you. It takes a great deal of courage to do that, but you may all be able to move forward afterwards.

Keeping calm

When communication breaks down or becomes disjointed everyone will lose out.

Sometimes, despite your best efforts, the difficulties between you and the other parent may seem insurmountable. It is even more important to remain positive and calm, otherwise you could jeopardise whatever tenuous thread of contact you may have.

One father gave the following practical advice for dealing with difficult situations:

> ➢ Keep calm/never ever answer back.
> ➢ Always be on time for contact pickup and drop off.
> ➢ Avoid becoming angry no matter how provoked.

- ➤ Where possible, arrange the hand-over of children on neutral public ground.

- ➤ No matter how tempted, do not express resentment of mother in front of children.

- ➤ Always remember to focus on being a loving father and not a resentful ex.

- ➤ Discreetly make notes of ugly scenes and unreasonable behaviour, with witnesses if you can, and keep a diary of events. This may be needed if things don't improve and you think your children are suffering.

- ➤ Use "141" facility when ringing for contact (less excuse not to answer your call).

- ➤ Contact another FNF member for support if feeling suicidal or like giving up.

- ➤ Never give up in the view that it is better for the child – it is not!

It is sad, but realistic to have to think of future repercussions should things go wrong, and you need proof of reasonable or unreasonable behaviour (of either parent). You must also be aware that your behaviour can easily be misinterpreted, and if judged as aggressive or angry, this may raise questions about your ability to look after your children. Take the advice in the next section very seriously.

WALKING ON EGGSHELLS

The time when children are collected or are taken back to the other parent can be stressful. It may be one of the few times that parents meet face to face. Inevitably, each will be tense, anxious perhaps to raise issues that need discussing. More worrying are the times when tempers flare, and one parent or the other will be determined to score a point.

It is crucial to keep calm at these moments. Although it can be difficult when you have to deal with your own emotions, *focus on the children*. If either parent ends up shouting or swearing, the children will be upset, possibly frightened. Abuse such as *'They know you don't care about them'* can become a regular feature of the 'doorstep conversations'.

Children with their weekend carrier bags in hand are unable to escape although often they learn to ignore it. Attempting to undermine the relationship with their other parent unnecessarily damages their self-confidence and causes anxiety.

Ironically, if the 'resident' parent gets angry with you, this is seldom perceived as causing problems for children. However, any behaviour on your part that can be interpreted as aggressive, including appearing angry, places you at risk of not being allowed to have contact with your children (FCWS p80).

Any behaviour likely to be interpreted by a court as intimidating may be sufficient to convince the court to make an order against you. Often no evidence of actual violence is necessary: it is sufficient for the other parent to state they are/were afraid. This is especially relevant for those who are still living in the same home. Courts have wide-ranging powers to deal with family violence. You may find yourself ousted from your home, and can be ordered not to go near your family.

Many FNF members report that professionals who may become involved (police, social services, health professionals, the FCWS etc.) commonly seem to work from the presumption that it is the woman who needs protecting. This happens even when the children's mother has initiated a domestic incident and been abusive and/ or physically violent. One father although abused and attacked on numerous occasions by his ex-partner, was sent literature asking him if he would like counselling for 'his' problem.

Where a mother refuses contact, negative assumptions may also be made about the past behaviour of the father.

"He must have done something to give her cause for concern about the children."

Although this ought to be unacceptable without evidence, in reality you will be the one who will have to prove your innocence. You *must* proceed with caution when dealing with a parent who is resisting contact, or the professionals who may become involved. For example, it is simply common sense not to go into the other parent's home on your own. Also make sure you have someone with you who can act as a witness if needs be.

If contact with the other parent results in confrontation, it is probably a good idea to work out other ways for the children to move between parents, to reduce the conflict for all.

"Try collecting children at a neutral venue. This is more natural than one parent 'taking' the children 'from' the other. It is normal to take or collect from school (make sure the school is aware).

This avoids contact, possible conflict between parents. Even if parents are trying to work everything out for the children's sake, they may not be very friendly to each other."

Other members suggest arranging the 'transfer' via a child-minder or at a mutual friend's home. Meeting in a public place such as a supermarket or McDonalds can also reduce the likelihood of arguments – very sensible advice, if all are able to recognise the damage that can be done when children witness angry scenes. The biggest problem, as with all disputes between parents, is that one parent may have more power to control what happens. They may not want to change existing arrangements. If they refuse to co-operate, you have limited options.

Possible solutions

You could ask someone they trust to help you resolve the problem, perhaps a member of their family, a friend, a representative of their religious group. Some members of FNF have mediation or counselling experience and may be able to offer advice. You could try a mediation service (Mediation/conciliation p9). Local FNF members may be able to suggest which ones have been helpful.

If you have to seek legal advice, go with a firm idea of what you want to achieve, i.e. less conflict for all, especially children, and not an aggressive and protracted legal battle. This will only make the lawyers rich, and make others more determined to 'win' (also see Part Three). Prepare a schedule that would result in fewer problems for children. FNF may be able to help with this.

Ultimately, you must convince the court that you are concerned about the effects upon the child and as such are trying to improve current arrangements. It is acknowledged that those hearing such applications, having to make decisions where families cannot agree, do not have any magic solution to contact problems. They are therefore faced with difficult decisions. Time allowed for hearings or the preparation of welfare reports (FCWS p80) is rarely sufficient to explore background history or problems,[1] or the options available, therefore any positive input on your part must be beneficial.

Freedom and risk

It can be extremely difficult to differentiate between personal feelings about what environment, company you would *prefer* your child to be in, and what is

---

1 There are extensive powers to check information held by other agencies, e.g. the police. Be prepared for anything alleged to count against you.

actually harmful. When there is little or no real communication, there is much scope for misinterpretation of motives and reality. The 'truth' is often difficult to establish.

It is easy to over-react, perhaps by finding the slightest excuse to reduce contact, or even deciding to apply for the children to live with you. It is easy for mums or dads to become paranoid about the other parent's inadequacies.

> "I 'disapproved' of the way she'd over-react to every sniffle, yet when I knew my child was at risk, no one would take me seriously."

'Good enough' is good enough: don't expect perfection. Every parent makes mistakes, but it is more constructive to focus on what they positively contribute to the lives of their children. Being constantly critical is destructive and influences children adversely. It may undermine their relationship with their other parent and anyone else they share time with in that parent's home, e.g., new partners, step-parents, other children (New partners p62).

Although it is sometimes hard not to feel possessive about children, *they must feel free to keep in contact with both their parents and the rest of their family*. It is this freedom that is infinitely more important than how much time they spend with each parent, or even the 'quality' of that time spent together.

MAKING THE MOST OF TIME TOGETHER OR APART

Whatever your situation, maintaining a relationship with children after you and the other parent no longer live together is far from straightforward. It is natural to want to make the most of the precious time with children not seen very often. This does not mean that they have to have a 'mega' experience every time they 'go to Dad's'. It can be difficult to strike a balance.

> "Don't rush them. Learn to just relax with them. Do nothing, sit around, watch TV. So-called 'quality time' isn't just about having fun."

The most important aspect is the relationship between you and your children. It may be the most basic things you will do together that build a lasting memory. One dad was living in a rented flat without a washing machine (fathers often end up in poorly equipped accommodation). When his young son came to stay, they would go to the launderette, put the washing in the machine, then sit eating fish and chips on a wall outside. Not exciting stuff, but years later his son often asks,

'Do you remember when we used to go to the launderette?' He sees this as the good times spent just with his dad.

Accommodation

When you first divorce or separate from the other parent, a decision has to be made about the division of the (often limited) family assets. Many fathers assume they have no alternative but to move out of the family home, are even advised to do so by solicitors. FNF would generally advise them not to move out, especially if arrangements for children to stay in contact with both parents have not been worked out. It may even be presented as desertion and count against you later. Accommodation for children is the first priority, as it should be, but their housing needs do not necessarily require only 'one base'. The pattern of life will be different for everyone after parents eventually move apart. If children are to continue to have both parents fully involved in their lives, they will need to spend time with both parents, in their respective homes. They can and do adapt to moving between their two bases.

Being able to have your children to stay with you is essential if you are to keep your relationship intact. It is seldom acknowledged that many fathers cannot afford suitable accommodation for their children after families split up. Taking children to McDonalds or out for a pizza is easily perceived as spoiling children, and can cause friction especially if the other parent is unable to afford to do this. But catering for children is a real problem when living in a bedsit. Not having room for children to stay overnight also seriously limits the amount and quality of time together. They will need their own space, however basic, with both parents. Put forward the argument that children are less likely to have satisfying contact – and may even be denied it if there is not suitable accommodation for them to stay with you (FCWS p80). If a court orders that there should be one 'main' home, the costs incurred by the parent travelling to and from that home should be taken into account. If maintenance is calculated under the Child Support Act (p59) no allowance is currently made for these essential costs. Reforms due to take effect (for new cases) by April 2002 indicate that the parent paying child support will be able to apply for a reduction if they have *'exceptional contact costs'*.

Being realistic, mothers will probably assume that children should live with them. The need for you to provide (and fund) additional accommodation elsewhere may not be taken on board. They may feel insecure about their own housing needs, how they will manage financially. It is hard to come to terms with the fact that standards of living will drop, as they inevitably will when parents split up. Both parents need time to adjust to their new situations. At such times, it is difficult to focus on the needs of the children. However, *if all round responsibility can be shared between you, there are obvious benefits for all, especially your children.*

Children's possessions, etc.

What happens about their toys, clothes etc.? You may be reluctant to let them take these to their other home. Older children especially may resent any interference – a gift is not a gift if there are conditions attached. It's probably better not to be too rigid about most things. If you decide that you would prefer some major items to remain at your home, explain that it's not practical to keep buying replacements, and they will need some familiar things at your home and something to play with next time they visit or stay over. You can always re-assess the situation if it doesn't work out.

Clothing is a more complex issue. Who buys what for where causes lots of ill-feeling. It is not unheard of for children to arrive for a fortnight's stay with only one set of clothes. Keeping spare clothes specifically for wearing at your home is common sense. Be sure to return any clothing that your child brings in good condition. You will not be popular if you send everything back unwashed unless, as reported by one father, the mother objected to the smell of the fabric conditioner that his new partner used. There will be times when you just can't win! Always remember to return other essentials such as homework and school items. Children frequently forget what they brought in the first place. If your relationship with the other parents is tense, you may get the blame. Children can also be very upset if they think they will be told off. One six-year-old became really anxious about returning exactly the same supermarket carrier bag his mum had used for his clothes. There have been many cases where contact was stopped following an argument over something comparatively trivial.

Distance between homes

The distance between you and the other parent is obviously going to play a major part in how you arrange to share responsibility, and organise time with children. Many parents will complain bitterly that their children have been moved from North London to South London, necessitating a trip across the Thames. Others accept with equanimity a move from London to Norwich or Birmingham as awkward, but not too unreasonable.

It really is a question of what you can manage, what you are prepared to do to keep the relationship with your children active. Many, many FNF members travel vast distances, regularly. They do this simply because they are parents, couldn't imagine being anything else. The expenses and time involved shape their lives, often leaving them very short of money. New partners may be unable to deal with the commitment and stress. Keeping in contact is expensive: poorer fathers often just cannot afford the costs involved. There is however, little recognition or sympathy for relatively poor dads.

When children are moved away

Travelling between homes within the UK, or indeed anywhere, becomes more of a problem when the long weekend visit becomes untenable. When it is first discovered that the 'ex' intends to take the children off to live somewhere else, the immediate reaction is *'Surely they can't do that?'* Unfortunately, despite the principles in legislation concerning children (Legal framework, p71) they almost always can, and this fact is one of the most poignant examples of the inequality between mums and dads.

If persuasion against such a move has failed, the objecting parent can (some would say, should) apply for a court order preventing the move. The other parent may apply to the court to remove the children *'from the jurisdiction'* (outside England and Wales). The court will probably still give permission for permanent removal of a child from the jurisdiction if proposals can be shown to be 'reasonable' and 'realistic', and are consistent with the child's welfare. The court has wide discretion, and should take the views of older children into account. However, UK case law (past court judgements) shows that mothers are almost always given leave to take children to live abroad, even though contact with their father is made difficult or even impossible. One very young child was taken to live in the USA. Her father who lives in the UK was granted *'not more than one extended weekend per month'* (e.g. Friday, Saturday and Sunday), and *'not less than two hours on each weekend day'* – all to take place in the USA. Any further contact is *'subject to reasonable negotiations between the parties'*.

So far he has been unable to re-negotiate this arrangement and therefore spends many hours travelling back and forth across the Atlantic every month to be with his daughter for just a snatch of time.

The legal situation here is some way off that in other countries where greater emphasis is placed upon sharing responsibility and care, and where *both* parents have to respect the children's right to a continuing relationship with their family.

Holidays overseas

If you do not have PR, you will have to get the other parent's permission for anything concerning your children, including holidays abroad.

If you have Parental Responsibility and there are no other orders in force then you have equal legal status with the mother and can in theory take your children anywhere you like on holiday. However, it is an offence for any person to take children out of the UK without 'appropriate consent' (Abduction Act, next section). It makes sense and can avert possible misunderstandings if you get prior agreement.

If you have a Residence Order (p72) in your favour, you can take the child out of the UK for up to one month without seeking consent. However, anyone else who has PR can apply for a Prohibited Steps Order (p72) to stop you, if they choose to do so (also see Abduction below).

If there is a Residence Order in favour of another person then you cannot take children from the UK unless you have the written consent of that person and every other person who has PR or have obtained leave of the court, e.g. by Specific Issue Order (p72).

Abduction

The Child Abduction Act 1984 makes it an offence to take or send a child out of the UK to live abroad without the appropriate consent from everyone who has PR for the child or leave of the court. The maximum penalty for a conviction is seven years' imprisonment.

If your child is taken to live abroad without your consent or in breach of a court order, you may apply for a return under the Hague Convention on International Child Abduction, if a contracting state is involved. A return will enable you to have the case heard in the UK courts.

If you fear an international move, it is vital that you immediately apply to a British court to establish jurisdiction. If you do not and the move is presented as a permanent one, the children may be deemed to be habitually resident in their new country almost immediately. You may find it very difficult to mount a case for residence and contact in a court overseas. These are highly technical matters, and *if you think this might happen to your family, immediately contact the relevant voluntary or government body best equipped to give you specific advice* (Part Four: Nos 4 & 18).

Practical considerations

However the move overseas comes about, whichever route you choose to resolve the problems, children will want to see you just as much when they find themselves in Bolivia as when they were still up the road. The logistics of maintaining the contact become entirely dependent on money, time available and co-operation. If co-operation is happening, then costs and travel can be shared, together with telephone calls and incidentals like passports, visas, etc. Young children need to be accompanied when travelling and this burden is halved if both parents pitch in. You will need information about what you can and can't do legally and what welfare benefits are available (start with the Citizens Advice Bureau).

> "People need basic information about 'unaccompanied minors' on aeroplanes, risks of unaccompanied travel in general, child fares on transport, cheap telephone accounts for international calls, family railcards, best bed & breakfast guide, possibly get a camper van if children are still in the UK, getting child benefit if the ex is abroad, in my experience use Virgin airlines because they have the best approach to kids and individual TVs for each seat, essential when kids want to watch something nobody else wants or can't see the big screen over the top of the seat in front etc., etc."

As this shows, the increasing numbers of FNF members who have children living abroad are undoubtedly the best people to ask about all the practical details. They report that airlines, for instance, are increasingly geared up to children travelling alone and children actually enjoy the independence.

As said before the prospects of stopping a move abroad are slim. Some would therefore advise negotiating as good a deal on contact time, costs and child support as possible. This can save everyone costly and counter-productive legal action.

With hostile ex-partners, where no negotiation is possible and the object of moving may be to disown the other parent, then the situation is dire as the following account shows:

> "I tried to get her to go to mediation in the USA (which costs $200 an hour plus the cost of drawing up a mediation agreement at the end – I offered to pay) to sort out the

34

contact situation. My ex said that she was not interested in mediation. I had actually booked a whole week in the States in August, to allow time for mediation, only to be told afterwards that she wasn't interested. As I couldn't change my ticket, I had to spend the time there but wasn't allowed to see my daughter one minute over the minimum time allocated by the court."

If circumstances allow, it may be easier for you to move too. This may seem drastic, but on the plus side, the legal system in countries like Australia and *some* parts of the USA[2] are more father-friendly and the chances of obtaining contact are greater. Always make sure you check the most up-to-date local information about the system in whatever countries or regions apply in your situation.

Indirect contact

When all else fails or the distance between you and your children is a major problem, indirect contact can keep the relationship alive. Do all you can to try to prevent them being distanced from you. Some hostile parents will block even this form of communication. *You may not be confident that children will receive your letters, but write anyway. Keep copies, so that in the future you can reassure them that you didn't just give up.*

Don't expect children to write you thank-you letters for presents and so on. They don't usually spontaneously write anything – or say 'thank you' – until they are quite old, unless an adult encourages them. If you do not get a thank-you, it is not the child's fault. It does not mean they are not pleased to have your messages and gifts. And if they write, or say that they do not want to hear from you anymore or to have your presents, etc., it may be because they have been told to do this. This reflects the difficult position they are in (Parental alienation p66).

Even young children may suspect all is not quite right, and actually resent the invasion of their privacy.

"I remember thinking that she (Mum) had a cheek opening my letters. Think she was afraid of him (Dad) saying anything that might set us against her. He never did – just used to ask how she was. Dad was determined: he never missed my birthday. He told me to phone and reverse the charges."

2   Legislation varies from state to state: attitudes and practices will be different in each one.

You could try phoning regularly, but again it is easy to prevent calls getting through, simply by leaving the answer machine on (try dialling 141 first).

"It was hard to do because I really wanted to know what was being said but, I used to encourage my children to ring their mum, and I made sure I was out of earshot while they did. Parents should allow their children privacy to contact the other parent."

It is not easy to be relaxed when speaking to a child you may not see often, and they may not be able to speak freely either, if someone is listening. If they seem distant, it isn't because they don't want to hear from you. Their priorities are different. You may have called in the middle of the favourite TV programme, or when their friends are with them. If they live in a different country, phoning across time-zones is particularly difficult, especially if you don't know what activities, etc. they are involved in. However, it can be relatively inexpensive to call long distance: find out what deals are currently available.

You could buy them a phone card or even a mobile phone if you can afford it. This does make things a bit less complicated for them. Don't be disappointed if they don't often ring: at least they have the opportunity. Computers are greatly improving the prospects for all to keep in touch. Children who would never ring or write may be more used to sending e-mail. They will probably be unsupervised for some of the time, so it is also a relatively private way for them to communicate with you.

There are many fathers who have had restrictions placed on their indirect contact with their children. They may be expected to phone only so many times in a given period, or at very specific times. Some have been ordered not to contact their children at all, even though they are decent, caring parents. This can happen when it is claimed that the other parent finds contact upsetting. It is 'justified' on the grounds that 'upsetting the mother might upset the child'. The fact that the child's relationship with its other parent might be damaged seems to be of lesser importance. If you are ordered indirect contact only, ask for a review after a short period to be built in. *If you cannot change things, continue to do whatever you can short-term, and focus on the hope of improvements. As your children get older, it will be easier for them to make their own decisions.*

It is perhaps also a good idea to take stock of what may be a comfortable routine for you, but perhaps no longer suits everyone else. Many have recommended regularly reviewing arrangements to adapt to children's and adults' changing needs and circumstances. Children often have strong views on this, but they can be the last to be asked. They may not be free to volunteer an opinion.

"She was told Dad wanted to reduce weekly contact to once a month because he didn't want to do all the travelling involved. She found out years later that it was Mum who made the decision, not Dad (Mum's new partner didn't like Dad appearing so regularly). She missed the weekly contact, but didn't say anything at the time, thinking Dad didn't care. Nobody thought to ask her. Even if they had, what would she have said?"

Research suggests that children desperately want to be informed. You should talk to them: be honest about what is happening and why, even if it appears to contradict what others are saying. That way, they can work things out for themselves. It might give them the courage to speak out if their views and feelings are not being considered.

PART TWO: *Being Realistic*

GETTING TO GRIPS

This section will touch on some situations you may have to deal with. *"I thought I was the only one..."* is a comment frequently made by newcomers to FNF. Working through some of the problems that can arise as you and the other parent try to re-shape your lives apart can be time-consuming, stressful and demoralising. Take comfort from the fact that others have had similar experiences and understand how you might react, and more importantly, have a more realistic idea of what you can and can't change. Hopefully, their insights may prepare you for some of the unknowns, and help you decide what's best for you and your family. FNF also has a series of guides and leaflets on a wide range of issues (see Part Four). The FNF local contact volunteers can also help.

The first thing to consider is how attitudes to men and childcare might affect your decisions. *It is a myth that men cannot look after children.* You will need to be prepared to challenge common assumptions, and perhaps your own views on what dads can do.

CARING FOR CHILDREN

When parents no longer live together, there is a major adjustment necessary, by all concerned. Each will have to adapt to having sole responsibility while the child is with them.

Be confident

Caring for children is often regarded as 'women's work'. *Men are often the first to believe this.* A dad recently said that he thought his wife was *'instinctively better'* at doing all the caring especially when his child was young. It could be argued (and was by his wife) that this has nothing to do with instinct, but simply the amount of time spent with either parent. This is also reinforced when Dad takes a crying child back to Mum to 'make it better'. Being seen as the parent with the magic wand is very satisfying. Women still assume the main caring responsibility for children within a relationship, often because they prefer to do so. That does not mean that men are not equally capable of performing the same tasks for children.

> "Michael has sole care of his three-year-old son. He works full-time, lives a fair distance from his work. He has no relatives nearby who might otherwise have helped. He therefore decided to find childcare facilities near where he works. His son spends the day at a nursery. Michael sees him at lunchtime, takes him to the park, etc. When they get home, Michael deals with all the other chores that need to be done."

Looking after children is not a magic science, just practice and determination to care as best you can for your children. *If you get it wrong sometimes, so what?* If there were a blueprint for raising children perfectly, the inventor would have made a fortune.

If you are unused to taking charge of all the aspects of childcare, don't panic! Get some advice, ask your friends, family: buy some magazines. *WHICH? Magazine*, Jan 2000 issue (available from reference section of main libraries) is a good starting point for anyone needing an overview of government policy, rights to free places, options, costs, who to contact for information, etc. Local authorities or social services can also help with what's available in your area. They keep lists of registered child-minders, nurseries, etc.

Sharing the care of children means that some dads have to re-assess and re-organise their working patterns. This is a good thing, allowing both parents an opportunity to broaden their input into their children's lives. Some may choose less demanding jobs, or work flexi-hours, so that they can be available when they are needed. Few employers have yet taken on board the concept of men needing childcare facilities, or time off when children are ill or to go to school events, etc. It isn't yet common practice for men to arrange their working lives around children, but it is improving as an increasing number of families have similar needs. It is illegal to discriminate by gender of parent. Employers must provide the same facilities for your children whether you are a mother or father.

Parental leave

In December 1999, new fathers were for the first time given a right to thirteen weeks' unpaid parental leave, to be taken during the first five years of the child's life (for employees with at least one year's continuous service). Leave for mothers was also amended.

The new rules allow parents of children born on or after 15th December 1999 to take time off work for family reasons until the child is five years old. The leave is available to all mothers, all married fathers, unmarried fathers who have obtained Parental Responsibility, and adoptive parents. If twins are born, each parent may take thirteen weeks leave for each child. Employees remain employed while on parental leave and are guaranteed the right to return to the same (if leave taken is less than four weeks) or similar job. Divorce or separation does not affect the right to take parental leave. As at December 2000, the government has proposed that all new fathers should have the right to two weeks' paid paternity leave. A decision is expected in 2001.

State benefits

Caring for children can be expensive. Both parents with care of children should check out the range of benefits. Find out what's available (the Citizens Advice Bureau should be able to help). While there are many state benefits available to parents, divorced or separated fathers often complain of difficulty in claiming them. The system is still geared to one 'primary carer' (usually presumed to be the mother, or whoever can prove he or she has the greater share of care). It seems to be an 'all or nothing' approach that is too inflexible to cope with the increasing number of children who have parents living in two separate homes. It is also geared to whole weeks of care, and only nights count. Therefore, if your shared care arrangements do not fit this pattern, for instance if your children are with you all day, but not overnight, you may lose out. However, don't be put off: if you think you should be entitled, make a claim. It can be a time-consuming process, convincing officials of your entitlement. Eventually, the system will have to adapt.

Some tax allowances (e.g. Children's Tax Credit from April 2001) can be shared between two households caring for children. You and the other parent (and possibly any new partners) will have to decide between you how you are going to share this Credit. If you are unable to do this, contact the Inland Revenue Helpline for further advice and information (Part Four: No 28). As a last resort, independent (from the IR) arbitrators will make the decision for you.

It is a good idea to get as much information as you can, preferably before you have resigned yourself to your child being brought up mainly by the other parent. Sharing the care, shares the responsibility, gives both parents more opportunities to work at the next step in their lives, move on.

43

Resistance

"I know hundreds of fathers and have yet to meet one who can't gently hold his child or change its nappies, whatever is needed. In cases where a father might need genuine help with managing his baby this can be provided much better in a setting where the emphasis is on enabling rather than controlling."

Unfortunately, not all you meet may see it quite like this. If you cannot agree about arrangements for sharing care, you will find that mothers are universally regarded as being 'entitled to contact'. Fathers are routinely expected to 'prove' they are fit to look after their children. There appears to be a general reluctance to trust dads with children. The younger the children, the more resistance you may encounter.

It is irrational to be so over-cautious. Every day, fathers look after babies. It is also common for very young children to stay with other members of the family. As said earlier *children are adaptable. They can quickly adjust to new routines, will move between their parents quite happily if encouraged to do so.*

You will not be able to persuade all that you are (still) a capable parent. Don't expect support even if you have previously been the sole carer. Presumptions about what is 'natural' are commonplace. The other parent may be the most difficult to convince. It is common for courts, the FCWS (p80), etc. to be influenced by the mother's fears. Sometimes the motives for resisting contact have less to do with apprehension over childcare issues, but more to do with insecurity, i.e. fear of losing the children, or the result of more negative motives such as revenge.

If there are doubts put forward about your ability to look after your children, the court may suggest that a relative or friend, or even a court welfare officer should be with you and your child during contact time. The place and time you meet may be clearly defined. It can be extremely traumatic to have to interact with your children under such artificial circumstances. It is also not ideal for them either.

"One Dad said that the *(maternal)* grandmother would not at first let him feed his baby. Eventually she did let him do so, but would check to see if he had washed his hands first. He persevered, and gradually was 'allowed' to take his child out for an hour or so (with granny in attendance). It was the mother who insisted that gran should be there."

Allegations of abuse

Domestic violence, and abuse of children are very sensitive issues. Children need to be protected when there is evidence that they are at risk. If you are a father, it can be difficult to convince the 'powers that be' that a mother is harming a child. You also risk upsetting what may already be precarious contact arrangements. The risk to the child is the first priority. First of all, be as certain as you can that the risk is real (Freedom and risk p28).

Sometimes allegations of misconduct, or abuse of either ex-partner or children are made where there is no evidence of risk, e.g. no history of abusive behaviour.

"My solicitor described allegations as routine."

This routine practice has also been described as 'the ultimate weapon', recognised within the legal system as a means to prolong the court proceedings, often after all other attempts to thwart contact have failed. If the court is concerned about risk to children, even where the 'evidence' is simply based on the word of a 'concerned' person, they must investigate claims made. Given that it is the duty of the court to protect children, there is a tendency to err on the side of caution.

Many such claims evaporate once investigated but they can still influence what happens afterwards. One father was suddenly accused of sexually abusing his child in the latter part of the divorce proceedings: the claims were not substantiated. The mother still insisted that a relation should temporarily supervise contact. Over a year later, this was still happening. He could go back to court but is concerned that this might cause more conflict, perhaps even less contact. He is therefore resigned to the current arrangements, hoping for improvements as the child gets older.

The many ordinary, decent, caring parents that have been falsely accused can testify to the damaging consequences especially for their relationship with their children. When the other parent is determined to stop contact, they may be tempted to use desperate measures. Be aware that an accusation might be made but don't become paranoid. *It is important to keep this in proportion, not let it interfere with what should be a relaxed and loving relationship with your children.*

If it does become an issue in your case, you must take it seriously. Just be aware that anything might be misconstrued, used against you.

"A father phoned to ask for advice about his very young daughter. When he collected the child for a contact visit, he was given some cream that had to be applied for nappy rash. The relationship between the parents was tense. He was in tears because he was terrified that by applying the cream, he might be accused of sexual abuse."

The advice he was given for his protection was to ask a female neighbour to treat the nappy rash, just in case his motives were misinterpreted. Fathers now routinely change nappies, bath their children, etc. This is encouraged, regarded as 'normal'. It is only when the relationship between the parents breaks down that motives may be questioned. It is really sad that this affects what is an everyday caring relationship between parents and children.

Sometimes a child's innocent and obviously unoriginal remark can fuel unfounded fears and prompt an over-reaction.

"A young child's parents were unable to agree about contact arrangements. Contact was being resisted, and Dad had applied for a contact order. One day the child was at nursery and said, 'Daddy's a b——d'. The mother later used this statement (with the nursery staff's support) to claim that the child didn't want contact with Dad. Eventually an expert was appointed to interview the child. The child was asked, 'What is the worst thing your daddy has done to you?"

The question should have been: 'Where did he pick up a phrase like that?' Clearly any investigations thought necessary should be done sensitively bearing in mind that children (especially young ones) are apt to repeat things without understanding meanings or implications. If asked leading questions, they often try to give the answer they think is expected of them. Children should not have to take responsibility for whether they 'want' to see their other parent. The innocent father and child above no longer have any contact. Having exhausted every avenue attempting to re-starting their relationship, he is now disillusioned and despairing. It is no consolation that all may have been done with the best intentions.

Undoubtedly, there should be a way to deal with these cases more equitably. However, faced with the reality of an investigation into your family, you will in effect have to prove yourself innocent, that your behaviour will not harm your children. This may be unacceptable to you, and therefore difficult to deal with. The first priority is to manage the situation in order to produce the best outcome for you and your children. Your understandable feelings of outrage at the injustice could be judged negatively. Any irritability on your part might be seen as a potential risk to your children.

The other reason for co-operating fully with those who may become involved is to make sure that the process takes as short a time as possible. Make it clear that you are concerned to make progress in order to resolve matters quickly. The longer you do not have contact, the more your children's relationship with you will be adversely affected. The younger your children are, the greater the risk of this happening. Strangely, there is an assumption that the younger they are, the less they need to see you. There is no social scientific proof that this is the case, or that one parent is less important to their development and well-being than the other. There is however, lots of research that indicates that fathers have a positive impact on their children's lives.

You may have to put up with a gradual re-introduction of contact where there have been periods of no contact. It is quite usual for courts to suggest a gradual build up of contact time in such circumstances, or where very young children are involved. Again, it may seem unnecessary to be expected to go through this process with your children. After all, many parents, mothers *and* fathers successfully care for children.

It really may be more a question of ensuring that the other parent's insecurities, etc. are reduced. If they are anxious or uncertain, this will rub off on the children. It may be better to go along with the procedure. If as some fathers have done, you are able to work out and suggest a plan of your own, this may persuade the court that your first concern is for your children.

"You may want to blank the other parent out of your mind altogether."

The experience of being under suspicion can leave deep wounds. Fortunately, many members are able to say that eventually, their children are free to have a more normal relationship with them. It is, however, worrying that suggestions that you may have harmed them, implanted in their minds when they were much younger, may never be quite eradicated. *'I don't want to talk about it.'* It may be a grey area that neither you nor they either choose to discuss, or feel you want to discuss.

CONTACT CENTRES

When parents cannot agree about contact, they may be referred to a contact centre. Increasingly it may be suggested as a route to break the deadlock, a halfway house to proper, independent contact. In some cases, the court may order contact to take place at a contact centre.

It may be hard to accept this arrangement, especially when there is no good reason why you and your children should not meet in more 'normal' circumstances. Remember, if having failed to resolve arrangements for children you are forced to ask the court to intervene, they will recommend whatever is felt to be in the children's best interest.

Contact centres provide a safe, neutral ground for children to meet their 'other' parent. If allegations of abuse of children are made, even where there is nothing to substantiate the claims, the court may decide that contact centres are a compromise, safeguarding children, *should* there be any risk. For those falsely accused of whatever misconduct, this is doubly difficult.

> "Many fathers are understandably horrified at the very thought of having to meet their children under such unnatural circumstances."

Centres may also be used *'... where concern has been expressed about the visiting parent's ability to care for a child during contact'* (National Association of Child Contact Centres[NACCC]). It can also be a way to re-start contact especially where trust between the parents has broken down. It is understandable that in some circumstances, e.g. if either parent was a recovering alcoholic, some assurance would be needed that he or she could cope.

> "Contact centres are keeping 2000 children each week in touch with their non-resident parent, a grandparent or a sibling" (NACCC).

That must be better than no contact at all. So what are the centres like? They are run by a variety of organisations such as church groups and the WRVS. Most are affiliated to NACCC (270 members throughout England, Wales and Northern Ireland). There is a Code of Practice, but each centre is independent.

The premises can vary from ancient church buildings to modern halls. Some have separate facilities for parents to wait whilst meetings take place, others do not. Hours vary too, limited by the premises and helpers available. Your experience therefore will depend largely on where you live, and the attitudes of those running the centre. Most centres provide a 'hand-over' service so that parents do not have to come face to face. This does have advantages, especially limiting children's exposure to any problems between their parents.

Those working at centres are mainly volunteers. They are there to help but not interfere. They are not there to judge, or to 'take sides'. Their main concern is to provide neutral ground for the children, to minimise conflict for them if at all possible. Basically, no one likes 'having to use' a centre, but many parents have commented that they appreciate the volunteer staff are generally doing their best.

It's not ideal, you may find it humiliating, it may be said not to be 'meaningful contact', but is it better than nothing? It's impossible to forget that we have to deal with the real world, not how we know it should be. One father described what the experience was like for him. He hadn't seen his baby son for months: the mother refused all contact. Contact was eventually ordered to be at a contact centre in order that father and son could get to know one another again. Dad, although disappointed and nervous said:

"I had to start somewhere, and could deal with it as long as it was only short-term. After all, if there's nothing else…"

He and his son met for an hour each week, increasing to two hours after three months. He found it difficult and stressful because the mother would stay in the room (this centre had nowhere else for mums to wait). If the baby cried, she would take him home. However, he said that the volunteers at the centre were really sympathetic to fathers, and although they couldn't interfere in any way, they did eventually persuade Mum to stay downstairs. After six months, the order was reviewed. Mum still wanted to use the contact centre, but the court ordered that Dad could take his son home. The relationship between the parents is still a problem, but he now plays a part in his son's life.

Some dads find that all does not work out quite like this, but are still prepared to do whatever it takes in the long-term interests of their children. One travels from Europe every two weeks to visit his children at a contact centre. All previous arrangements had proved so unpredictable that it seemed the better option. Approximately two-thirds of families who try contact centres move on to more 'normal' contact afterwards. Other parents, however, are still meeting their children in this limited environment years later.

When this is happening because one parent is determined to impose conditions on the ongoing relationship between children and the other parent, life can be unpleasant for all, including the children. There will be no opportunity for anyone other than that parent to explain what is happening and why they have to meet Dad at a contact centre. Why isn't he allowed to take them outside, or worse, why can't he be trusted? NACCC has produced an excellent book to help children (Part Four: No 36).

Contact centres have a part to play in helping some children. The input by the dedicated volunteer contact staff has to be appreciated. Some contact may be preferable to none, *if there is no viable alternative.* However, the ultimate aim must be to keep this interlude as short as possible. Children should be able to resume a more relaxed relationship with those that care for them with the minimum delay.

The following might help you decide what to do if contact at a contact centre is proposed in your situation.

You may be able to convince everyone that it is not necessary. You will have to prove to the court, and especially the mother, that your intentions and behaviour are beyond reproach, and that you are capable of looking after your child. It sometimes helps if you can show you have the support of the child's grandparents.

If you fail on any of these points, and supported contact is ordered, build in a review after a short period, and/or put forward a plan to gradually move to more natural contact over an agreed time-span. Make this part of the agreement if you can.

It is important to be seen as willing to co-operate, but meeting at a centre should be a short-term compromise.

If, eventually, you find what is suggested or ordered unacceptable, and if there is no other way to see your child, consider carefully what not agreeing to this will mean for your relationship with your child. Be warned that if the alternative is not seeing them at all, you will have little opportunity to talk to them about anything, let alone explain how much you care about them. One father sums up how he coped as follows:

> "The main advice I would give any father or mother in similar circumstances is to make sure to keep up whatever little contact they can get, however difficult. The child will see this and respect them for it, and as time goes on and the child gets more and more say in his or her own life, things will gradually improve."

Children have to go along with whatever adults and the system decides for them. This does not mean that they should accept contact centres as a normal part of life. No one has yet to come up with all the answers to the problems when families break down. Given an opportunity and the approval of those around them, what would children choose? You may have limited choices too, so at least you understand how they feel.

A message from Eunice Halliday, the Director of NACCC:

> "It is important for non resident parents not to feel a failure because they are seeing their child at a contact centre. It is an indication of how hard they are trying to be there for their child...we know that many parents find coming to a centre a major ordeal."

Think long-term

Such precautions are seldom taken in 'ordinary' families yet, despite all the mistakes made every day, children seem to survive regardless. You may therefore think that what is required of you simply because you no longer live with the other parent is unreasonable, and feel resentful. Attitudes and practices are gradually improving things for fathers but in the meantime, you have to make the best of what can seem a very poor deal.

The over-riding advice from past and present FNF membership is *be prepared to compromise in the short-term if it will help you realise your long-term aim.*

SUPPORTING CHILDREN

When children live mainly with the other parent, how do you continue to play a part in their lives? Without up-to-date information about, for example, their progress at school, health problems, or simply what interests they have, who their friends are, you will be less able to help, less involved in their lives.

> *If you can, come to an arrangement on sharing information with the other parent at a much earlier stage, before any contentious issues crop up.*

Consider having a written agreement drawn up as proof that you both wanted to work together for your children's sake. It can be useful to re-focus attention on the importance of co-operation and the benefits to your children, if all does not go smoothly in the future.

If there is minimal or no communication between the two homes and no agreement, getting information may present problems. Realistically, when lives diverge to this extent, it is probably best to deal directly with those (schools, medical staff, etc.) who come into contact with your children. This can save time and avoid conflict, if handled sensitively.

Getting information about your children

If you have PR, you can make independent decisions for your children when they are with you, and you should be given information that affects them. It may be up to you to ask for the information. How you ask can make a big difference. The lack of knowledge relating to the legal rights and responsibilities when parents no longer live together is widespread. Even if you find out what the legal position is, do not expect others to either know or understand. This can result in many situations where you are refused information about your child, or even treated as if you present a threat.

The legal position also varies across the various professional fields. It would seem logical for responsible parents to have up-to-date information about the medical condition of their children, especially young children. If you have PR you have a right under the Data Protection Act 1998 to ask for such information, and the majority of parents will be granted access to medical records. However, doctors can limit or deny access in some circumstances, e.g. if they consider the information might cause serious harm to the physical or mental health of the child (or any other person).

> It can be frustrating to be told by a doctor that he will not let you see your child's medical records.

> It can be humiliating to be told by the school secretary that you can't speak to the child's teacher unless she checks that the other parent doesn't object.

> It can be alarming to be told by the hospital receptionist that they can't give you information about your child's progress because you are not the 'resident parent'.

All the above examples are common: you will have to learn to deal with this and much more. It is not a personal attack on your character. The Department for Education and Employment (DfEE) has issued clear guidelines to schools (Part Four: No 25). These explain whom they should involve in issues concerning a child's education. For the purposes of education legislation, this includes all natural parents, whether married or not, plus anyone else who has PR for the child (providing there are no court restrictions in place). Private schools do not have to follow these guidelines, but many probably will. Don't expect practices or attitudes to change overnight. All will take time to filter through, and you may still meet resistance. You may still be told that the school can't send you information, regular school reports, newsletters, etc. because of the extra costs.

The DfEE view has always been that both parents are entitled to receive the same information, but it is not unreasonable for schools to decide initially to give the information to one parent and to encourage them to share it with the other. This saves time and effort and of course conserves resources. If for whatever reason you do not get the information or it arrives too late for you to attend school events, explain this to the school. They should arrange to send the information directly to you (unless there is a court restriction in place). They should not treat one parent more favourably, but if you can afford it, it might be helpful to provide a supply of stamped addressed envelopes. This ensures that they send you what both parents need to know.

Change of name

Some fathers seeking information about their children are concerned when they discover a different surname is being used in school records. Courts accept that surname changes are rarely in the interests of children. A child's surname is legally protected where a Residence Order is in force. Any father with Parental Responsibility has a right to be consulted over a change of name by deed poll. A married father can apply for a Prohibited Steps Order to prevent a change of name. An unmarried father can apply for a Specific Issue Order to determine the surname by which the child should be known. Also be aware that an unmarried father's name cannot be entered on the birth certificate without consent of the mother, unless there is a court order in force (also see Court Orders concerning children p72).

It is not uncommon for a mother to try to change a child's surname after separating from the father, particularly where the couple were not married. Following divorce, she may ask the school to change a child's name in its records, perhaps to her maiden name. There are many arguments put forward for making such changes. When a mother re-marries, she may claim that the child will benefit from changing to her new surname, because s/he will feel less 'different' especially if there are other siblings.

As said earlier, divorce affects over one in four children by the time they are sixteen. The incidence of non-married parents splitting up is even greater. Children are therefore very likely to know others whose parents have split up and re-partnered. It is not such an issue for them as it may be for adults. It is actually very important for them to be in touch with their own identity. Pressing ahead with a name change, especially if there is disagreement, may also result in them feeling confused or guilty. It can also cause problems with schools and other authorities. The recent DfEE guidelines advise schools to be cautious about changing names in school records, without evidence – independent of the parent seeking to make a change – that all with PR had given their consent.

"The clearest evidence would, of course, be something in writing from the 'other parent' giving consent to the change..."

(p5 of the DfEE guidelines).

This should make it simpler for all to understand the legal implications. Without a change in current law, there is really no scope for individual interpretation, however well intentioned the motives may appear.

Even if the other parent objects, you should be kept up to date with all aspects of your children's school, including annual and other events. Ask politely for the information. If necessary, e.g. if the school secretary isn't helpful, write or make an appointment to see the head-teacher. You can refer to the DfEE guidelines, but be careful how you approach this.

> *The emphasis should be on the benefits of your involvement for your children.*
> *'It's my right to have this information' may just antagonise.*

There is a risk of upsetting your relationship with these professionals, and perhaps that between you and the other parent (which could adversely affect arrangements for children). However, persevere without becoming belligerent. It is even more important to do so if contact is being resisted. If you can get the school to understand the problems and to work with you, it can be one way of keeping in touch with children when all else fails. It sends out a clear message to children that 'the school' supports your role in their lives.

Clearly, in an ideal world, there should be support in place to prevent this kind of situation developing in the first place. Not many seem prepared to challenge parents resisting contact. To be realistic, the school's main concern is with education. As long as children appear to be OK, e.g. are not obviously showing signs of distress or physical abuse and crucially, are not presenting any behaviour problems, not too many questions will be asked about life outside school.

Open days, parents' evenings, etc.

Some parents are able to present a united front at least for school events. This is a good example for children if achievable. However, there are all kinds of issues that can lead to problems. If, for example, either or both parents find new partners, the resentment if they also want to show an interest in children's progress can be tangible.

Again, in an ideal world all could work together, play their respective parts in the children's lives. Children are uncomfortable if adults cannot control their own negative feelings towards each other. If you think that meeting the other parent is going to be difficult especially for your children, it is better to visit school separately. If you can discuss this with the other parent, there will be fewer misunderstandings: all will understand that the arrangements are for the benefit of the children. The children should also be involved in the discussions, so that they can understand that you are trying to do the best for them.

Unfortunately, the 'separateness' of parents' lives after family breakdown may not be appreciated by all. To be fair, schools are on *'slippery ground'*. They have little time to grasp all the legal issues surrounding contact with children, and they neither want nor should become involved in what appears to be a 'battle' over children. Teachers may hear two different versions of events. Don't be drawn into countering petty accusations that may be made. Conducting yourself with dignity and restraint, and remaining focused on what you can do to help your children will earn more respect.

Teachers are more used to dealing with the parent with whom the child lives most of the time, and are unlikely to question motives. They may not realise that feedback about school is not being passed to the other parent. If you still feel you cannot make headway, you can, of course, complain to a higher level, the head-teacher, the governing body and, after that, the DfEE. Be warned though, if all develops into a war between you and the school, it may actually not help your main aim, which is of course to play a meaningful role in your child's life. Again, you are advised to be polite, but firm.

Get involved

If you can become involved with some aspect of school life, perhaps by supporting the sports teams, joining the Parent Teacher Association (PTA) to help raise funds, you will also be seen as an 'interested parent' (this may be crucial if at some point legal proceedings become inevitable). Networking with other parents will also be helpful. Even young children will develop a social circle that can involve their parents in outings and activities – not to mention the birthday party circuit – where the children can interact and play with their friends. You can learn a great deal about what's happening at school, how your child is coping, what their interests and friends are like.

The main benefit is to your children, who will appreciate your interest. If you've actually met 'Teacher' or know what the classroom looks like, where their seat, desk, whatever is, you will both be more able to talk about their school life. It can cause problems for all concerned, if the other parent does not encourage your involvement.

"A father volunteered to go on a school trip with his daughter's class: extra adults were needed to supervise the children. The mother told him that if he did, she would keep the child away from school."

Irrational though this may sound (and given that the mother was a primary teacher herself), this is an example of a common dilemma. Unless you do what the other parent wants, she or he will create problems for the children, which you will be blamed for. What to do about it? There are no absolute rules, because no one wants to cause unnecessary conflict for children. However, backing off is not always the best thing for them long-term, since it's probably only reinforcing the other parent's ability to prevent your involvement. *It is crucial to remain involved, for your children's sake.*

It can be soul-destroying having to battle against such opposition, to gradually build up confidence in those who should not question your child's right to your support. Attitudes *are* changing, but it is a slow process. Much depends on the individuals you have to deal with.

> There is a great deal of evidence that parental involvement is crucial, not only for success, but for all-round personal development, including self-esteem. Don't doubt whether it's worth persevering.

Maintenance

Children need support (not just financial support) from their parents. This support is best provided when both parents are involved in their lives. Sharing care of children, spending time with them, gives both parents a greater understanding of their needs and an opportunity to choose appropriate essentials or presents. This is especially important when as is inevitable for many families, parents are not able to communicate, or one or both refuse to co-operate. Being instructed to simply pay up, without perhaps having contact with, or information about children causes resentment.

Whatever the financial arrangements for children before parents lived apart, this becomes a major issue afterwards. There is still a 'let's get the maximum out of this for our side' approach to the division of family assets. There may be precious few assets to share in some cases, increasing the pressure as living standards inevitably fall for everyone.

☛ "It is a fact that most contact disputes are ultimately about money." ☛

If the CSA (p59) is not involved, you can both draw up your own agreement about financial responsibility for children. Include a plan for regular meetings to exchange information, and to discuss their changing needs. All are more likely to feel happy about expenditure if they are involved in the decisions. Unfortunately, it does not always work out so smoothly. You also need to be aware that if you do come to a 'voluntary agreement' this does not prevent later CSA involvement in some circumstances, e.g. if the other parent claims Income Support or if the agreement has not been made part of a court order. (Note that there may be changes in the light of reforms to the CSA.) You will need to make the payments via a bank or get a receipt. Make it clear that the money is for child support. If you do not, you could end up paying twice.

There are so many issues that can cause resentment, envy and suspicion. Children are drawn into these disputes and can have damaging examples set for their futures. Therefore, the best advice must be to consider how all this effects them. Whatever the disagreement between you and the other parent, children need protecting from the fallout.

Children under pressure

Don't be drawn into arguments about money in front of children. They will not fully understand all the complex issues involved. If for example, one parent claims the other doesn't pay, won't pay, isn't paying enough, this can lead to resentment and could seriously affect attitudes to the parent claimed to be selfish and uncaring.

> "My dad doesn't pay my mum enough maintenance. He doesn't care about me."

Children also dislike being used as messengers. It can be obvious that they have been rehearsed to ask you for something. It shouldn't be their responsibility. They have to face the other parent when they go home. If you don't agree to buy whatever it is, they will feel worried in case they get into trouble. *They really can't win.* It may be that you are quite happy and able to buy them whatever they have asked for, but should you just pay up? Some would advise not giving in because it encourages children to be manipulative, or to see Dad's role as just a 'cash dispenser'. Others would say pay a bit more if you can.

> "Err on the generous side financially if it means the difference between little or no contact and a more relaxed situation. It's amazing how easy contact becomes when you cough up!"

Not all parents will be able to afford to do this, especially when there are others also involved e.g. new partners, perhaps other children. It is difficult to please or be fair to everyone. Whatever your views, try not to forget how little children can do about the whole situation.

If the relationship between you and the other parent is tense, try to at least agree that it would be better for your children if you did not have to bargain in front of them. Arrange to meet if you can, to go through the issues causing concern. It may be that in your situation this is impossible. You could write explaining that you take your responsibility for your children seriously, do your best to support them, but may have different views on how to provide the support.

If you do not see children often, and have little chance to get to know what they may need, what their interests are, it can be almost impossible even to decide what would be an appropriate present. In the circumstances, you may prefer to save for their future, perhaps opening a more long-term bank account for driving lessons, or further education.

> Be warned that if you cannot agree on a way forward, there is a real risk that this will lead to less contact.

Responsibility

The vast majority of fathers would give their children *'the top brick off the chimney'* if they were free to do so. *Free to do so*: that's the key issue. Some fathers are not free to do so because they may be unemployed, or on low pay. Some fathers may want to support their children more freely, but are not allowed to see them often or at all.

One of the saddest developments is the numbers of young fathers being deliberately excluded from their children's lives, almost from the birth of the child. The mothers of these young men contact FNF. The whole family is desperate to love the child, even though in some cases, the young dad may not be able to offer much financial support. They are a far cry from the typical media image of 'feckless youths'. They need help to help their children. What can they do if the child's mother, often backed by her family, does not want their help (apart from maintenance, if they can afford it)?

Recent research has shown that fathers who spend more time with their children support them willingly: the involvement they have in their lives is a crucial factor. If you know what your children need, you will do your best to sort it out. If you know what they want, you can decide whether they should have whatever it is. It is unrealistic to expect parents no longer living together, with separate lives, perhaps new partners and children, to be able to always agree amicably about who should pay and how much for children in common. Current legislation locks such households together for a child's lifetime, encouraging envious and acquisitive attitudes that are so damaging for all concerned, especially children.

Research also shows that the majority of parents who can afford to do so, regularly and willingly pay maintenance for their children. Many pay money to the other parent even when they have a shared parenting arrangement with equal care of the children. The current formal system for assessing maintenance (following section) has received widespread criticism from mothers and fathers since it was set up. It has recently undergone yet more changes. FNF has submitted its own proposals that would be fairer to both parents and cause less conflict for children (see FNF website). However, until these concerns are taken on board, the advice must be to work with what you are legally obliged to.

Child Support Agency (CSA)

The Child Support Act 1991 was followed by the formation of the CSA. Before 1993, if parents could not agree about maintenance for children, this was largely decided by courts. Parents can still make their own arrangements unless the other parent begins to claim Income Support. If that happens, the CSA will decide how much maintenance has to be paid. The most recent reforms (Child Support, Pensions and Social Security Bill, July 2000) are due to come in by April 2002 and will mean radical changes to the existing system The old and new rules will undoubtedly co-exist for a period.

> "The computer system being developed for the CSA will deal with new child support cases by April 2002. Existing cases will be transferred when the Government is sure the new system is working well."
> *(Department of Social Security Press Release 00/222)*

As at the date of this publication, the 'old' rules still apply. If the CSA becomes involved, you have no choice but to pay. Make sure you check the assessment, because many are inaccurate. Be aware that you are liable to pay as soon as you receive the Maintenance Enquiry Form. This might pre-date the actual assessment when it eventually arrives by up to six months. Delays or mistakes in the assessment are common and can mean huge arrears building up. If you are challenging a decision, perhaps start saving a regular sum so that when you eventually find out what you owe, you are not overwhelmed by the amount claimed. Keep records of all money paid to the other parent for children, plus any allowable expenses such as travelling to and from work.

There is not scope in this guide to cover all CSA related issues. If the CSA becomes involved in your child-support calculations, you should get up-to-date information and advice. The NACSA website includes a spreadsheet where current likely liability can be calculated. The CSA have a National Enquiry Line and a comprehensive website. *Make sure you get the information you need* (Part Four: Nos.14, 21 & 37).

SUPPORT FROM THE WIDER FAMILY

Grandparents (and aunts, uncles, others who care)

Family breakdown also affects grandparents and other members of the family with whom children may have had regular contact. When children lose contact with one part of their family, they lose their heritage, the memories of that half of the family. A grandparent is someone they can turn to perhaps when their parents are preoccupied or unsupportive. The grandparents' home is more likely to be a haven where children are accepted without question, and where they learn more about their parents.

> *"If it weren't for my grandparents I wouldn't have known who my dad was."*

Where there is lost contact, the outcomes for the respective families can be very different. Whichever parent loses contact, it is likely that his or her wider family will not see children either. This is so stressful. Many grandparents in this situation are afraid they will be forgotten, even fear dying without seeing these children again. One grandfather sent a letter enclosing a photo of 'nanny and granddad' to a 'missing' grandchild asking, *'Do you remember us?'* He did not get a reply. Even though grandparents may be keen to help sort out the problems, they may not know what to do for the best, and be reluctant to interfere.

> *"What could we do? We were powerless."*

In contrast, the 'other' grandparents may find themselves playing a larger part in the children's lives. They too will offer emotional and financial support, in some cases they help by being child-minders. They may also worry about being drawn into a situation over which they have little control. The disparity between the two wider families can cause problems. It is only natural that one will feel left out, not valued. This may make communication between the two families difficult. However, although both sets of grandparents may be affected differently, they both have a practical role to play, can be a quiet voice of reason when all around are losing the plot. This can be helpful for children who find what's happening between their parents worrying. If there is still some stability, if practical solutions are put forward for resolving problems, it is a good example for everyone.

After all attempts to see his grandson had failed, a grandfather decided to write to the other grandparents. It was not an easy decision for him because the two families had not spoken since their children divorced years earlier. The other grandparents didn't write back, but soon after, the daughter-in-law rang to say she was bringing their grandchild to see them. The advice to grandparents is much the same as that to fathers:

> ➢ Don't make assumptions.
> ➢ Don't be discouraged: make opportunities to keep in contact.

Do try to remain in contact even if children don't visit anymore, or you feel unwelcome by the other parent. It takes a great deal of courage to face possible rejection. It's worth it if children continue to know that you still love them regardless of changes to the family situation. Send letters, cards, make phone calls, even if there is no response. It is important for the children to know you are still there, even if out of sight.

It is easy to overlook children's perceptions of what is happening, and their lack of power. Children shouldn't feel guilty for something they cannot control. They may not be old enough to travel alone, cannot make decisions about visiting their 'other' family. If they know that one parent does not support such contact, they are powerless to do anything, even perhaps to show that they would like to see you. They risk disapproval and arguments if they make a fuss, and will choose the easy route.

So, the adults must help them by reaching in to their lives to say, *'It's OK, we know you still love us, and we will always love you, no matter what.'* It's really not their fault. Sometimes it takes years for all to understand why something happened, to work out the motives and weaknesses of all concerned. The following is a message of encouragement from the Grandparents' Federation:

"Grandparents' Federation often receive letters saying that they now have contact after many years – so don't give up."

If you are not able to see your grandchildren, the Grandparents' Federation may be able to advise on the way forward (Part Four: No 11). Grandparents can apply for a Contact Order (and possibly other court orders) with leave of the court. Whilst in practice such applications are best made by the child's parent, there are cases where separate applications may be appropriate and possibly successful.

New partners

"My child is now calling someone else Daddy."

Discovering this strikes at the heart of the relationship between parents and children; it is threatening and stressful. It is normal to feel both angry and powerless, especially when combined with limited or no contact with children.

Children, even young ones, understand who their 'real' parents are. The strain of having to conform to whatever adults think they should call everyone can be a real problem for them, especially if they know they are upsetting one parent or the other. Ideally, all the adults involved should get together, to focus on what's best for children. They will need help to understand where everybody fits into the scheme of things, how each person can play a complimentary but different role in their lives. The focus should be on what is best for the children (i.e. what the children are comfortable with), not what the adults find expedient.

Such co-operation and child-centredness is unfortunately not always possible. The family regarded as the 'main' family will undoubtedly make most of the decisions. You may have different views, but your children need to get by in that family, and they will only do so by fitting in, adapting to their different circumstances. This is not being disloyal, and it does not mean they love you any less. You are their parent, why would they? *Nothing, not even calling someone else 'Dad', however painful that may be, can change the special link your children have with you.*

"She's not his mother."

It doesn't matter at what stage you meet a new partner, he or she may present quite a problem to your children, especially if the other parent is resentful. Even when arrangements for sharing in the care of children have been working reasonably smoothly for a good while, the routine is almost guaranteed to be upset. Children can feel jealous, left out, in second place. *It is a good idea to make sure you and they still have some time together, on your own.* It is always difficult to balance your loyalties to all concerned. You are, after all, 'allowed' a new relationship, and your children must be helped to understand this.

Advice for new partners:

> "Keep a distance from the kids, don't rush at them; try not to be too friendly. Let the children come to you. Their most likely reaction is 'Gawd...what's Dad (Mum) brought home?!' They are likely to be wary for a considerable time. Be studiously neutral about the 'old' one, and try not to replace him or her."

Again, if there is any way for all of you eventually to come together to discuss your respective roles in the children's lives, it may make a considerable difference to future relationships. An irrational dislike of the person now sharing the ex-partner's life can lead to all kinds of negativity and unfounded suspicions. If these feelings are never aired, the assumptions just get more absurd, and the misinterpretation of motives (especially concerning financial matters) can make life really difficult.

The other parent will need reassurance. They may be behaving aggressively, perhaps making it difficult for children to make contact. It takes a great deal of courage to make the first conciliatory move especially if you expect a rejection. If you can find a way to say that you still love the children, still intend to do all you can for them, it may make all the difference. Most important of all, you should all accept that you and your new partner want to share in their care, not take them away altogether.

Social attitudes *are* gradually changing as more and more fathers make it clear they don't just want to play a minor role in their children's lives. Despite this, after family breakdown it is still far more common for it to be assumed that children will live mainly with one parent (almost always the mother) and 'visit' the other parent. When a new partner moves in with a 'resident' mother, it may be claimed that the new 'family' will be disrupted if children continue to see their other natural parent. This fails to consider the effects upon children who would be faced with the prospect of having to give up a loved and loving parent. Undoubtedly there are many excellent step-parents, but the relationship between children and a step-parent can be difficult to negotiate. Divided loyalties can cause problems for all involved. Children may need extra support as they adjust to family changes, and at such times, it is even more important to preserve the stable relationship they have with you.

Talk things through with your children, especially as things change. This helps them to get a balanced view of what's happening. If you are lucky, they may share their own feelings and views with you too. You may be surprised how different their needs are to yours, and these should be considered. Be aware that they will not want anything shared in confidence to rebound on them.

Even if you find you cannot overcome resistance to others who play a part in their lives, children should not feel they have to take sides. They must learn to move forward, to form new relationships. They need your help and encouragement to be able to do this. It is so easy to be critical without good reason. You must of course speak out if there are serious concerns about their welfare. Otherwise, they should be free to benefit from both their environments.

IMPLACABLE HOSTILITY

All the advice so far about being positive, behaving reasonably, etc., works from the assumption that if you work hard enough, if you genuinely try to put your children's interests first, all will be fine.

In many cases, it is not fine. The attitudes and behaviour of some parents *is* hostile and negative, and they resist contact to greater or lesser degrees deliberately. It may be purely a question of personality and it is unlikely that personality will change. Undoubtedly, there are families where all possible avenues have been explored, and there is no reciprocal desire to co-operate.

Children growing up under such pressure are doubly at risk. They feel stressed by the conflict that inevitably happens whenever Mum and Dad meet, speak on the phone, etc. They also have to live with the knowledge that the parent with whom they live doesn't want them to see their other parent.

It is a Catch 22 situation for them. Even though they love both parents, they are not free to show their feelings. One parent may appear angry, upset, not speak to them if they mention, or visit the other parent. The guilt must be overwhelming. Many side with the parent with whom they must survive (Parental alienation p66). They are also powerless to influence what's happening, may feel guilty because they cannot prevent it.

"I couldn't do anything about it: I was only eight at the time."

This was a comment from a child who hadn't seen one of his parents for years, after a total and sudden withdrawal of all contact. Ironically, the legal advice to the father at the time was:

"Given the intransigent attitude of the mother, no court will enforce your contact order."

So it seems that the court was also powerless to stop this happening (at least that's what the solicitor advised). The father therefore decided to withdraw from the 'battle' because he thought it would spare the child unnecessary distress. Plainly, conflict at the time was reduced, but at the expense of their relationship: years later, they do not know one another. It's easy to be discouraged by negative or cynical advice and understandable to be worried by threats to reduce or deny contact. Don't be persuaded that giving up is in the interests of children, or that taking legal action is pointless. Much will depend on the court, the judge or magistrates (Using 'the system' p82). Courts are more willing to act these days, but still not willing enough.

If you are being denied contact, first try to establish the underlying reasons. Suggest using a mediation service (p9). Without clearing up any misunderstandings, there is less chance of resolving the situation quickly and amicably. If all attempts to reason fail, taking legal action is an obvious step when communication breaks down. Take action swiftly to prevent further damage to the relationship that has been suspended. It is unfortunate that there are no informal yet effective mechanisms in place to solve contact denial without recourse to formal and costly legal proceedings. Sometimes applications can spread out over many months, possibly years. *Even when the other parent's intransigent attitude is really obvious, and previous court orders have been blatantly broken, you may find that very few judges are willing to take the robust action needed to support your child's right to a relationship with you.*

During the proceedings, the contact denial is continued, further eroding the parent/child relationship. The longer you hesitate, the more likely it is that the other parent will establish a routine for the children that excludes you. The courts and those who may become involved are reluctant to upset this pattern. They may view your determination to continue to be involved as a threat to the children's stable life elsewhere.

> "I went through the whole court process over twenty times. I was always being awarded contact but it hardly ever happened. I asked for the order to be enforced and was told that 'no judge in his right mind' would use the sanctions available."

This reflects the very difficult choices that have to be made when considering outcomes for children. Again, if you can get everyone to *focus on the importance for the children of a continuing relationship with both parents*, they may be more prepared to deal more firmly with the parent who is preventing your involvement. Often, your intentions are misjudged, and you will be seen as 'wanting to exercise your rights' over your children. *It may be worth emphasising that your primary concern is to meet your children's need for maximum support from family and friends.*

Many men feel especially uncomfortable seeking help with private family matters, but it *is* worth contacting agencies that can mediate between you and the other parent. Never assume that your ex-partner will not co-operate. Sometimes an approach by a third party works, and can open up new channels of communication, suggest different ways forward. It has to be said that if the other parent is determined to stop contact, they may resist attempts to find a compromise, because they know this will inevitably mean they will have to 'give up' the children.

If you exhaust all avenues, but your children still lose contact with you, *you must not give up hope that things might improve later on. It has happened for so many people.* Meantime, keep records of what you tried to do to resolve the problems, to keep in touch. Include all the positive measures you took, the reasons why contact stopped. There's no need to be overly critical about the other parent. Be honest but stick to the facts. In time, everyone needs more information about the past. Those with only one part of their history will need to balance this out eventually with the other perspectives.

Parental alienation

There is a growing awareness that one parent determined to sever all contact between children and the other parent may begin to alienate children against that parent and also the wider family and friends. In extreme cases, this will result in children effectively rejecting part of their family (Parental Alienation Syndrome or PAS).

This is also the territory of false accusations, used sometimes to support claims that children are afraid, do not want to have contact.

"I wrote to my daughter often weekly, never less than twice a month, and I sent her presents continually, not only at birthday and Christmas-times. But I very rarely got any reply. Sometimes my letters and presents were returned unopened. When my daughter did write it was hate-mail, urging me to 'go away and leave her/ them alone'. Once or twice my daughter left hate-messages on my answering machine."

This is heartrendingly difficult to cope with. Many dads (and mums) in this situation refuse to give up, despite the sometimes overwhelming obstacles, especially doubts about whether their children really have stopped loving them. Don't let others, including, sadly, the practitioners who may get involved, persuade you to back off. When faced with these intractable situations, they may be afraid to challenge the behaviour of the 'main' parent, arguing that this might cause problems for the children. The easiest option will usually be to recommend that they remain with the alienating parent, even though this continues to jeopardise their relationship with the other parent. Although the term 'PAS' is widely recognised especially in the USA, you may find its use can antagonise, especially if you are representing yourself in court. If describing alienating behaviour, it may be better to use more familiar words such as brainwashing, or attempts to influence children against you.

Fortunately there are some experts who specialise in this field, who appreciate that parental alienation is deeply damaging for children and should be dealt with accordingly. FNF may also be able to steer you in the direction of sympathetic legal and specialist advice. It also produces a comprehensive guide to parental alienation and has extensive references to related literature on its website (also see Part Four: No 45).

Sadly, there are many fathers (and some mothers) living apart from children who know that their children are being turned against them. If you are fearful that your child has been misinformed about you, rather than focusing on the worst that may happen, go back over the earlier advice, and try to stay positive, never give up hope for change in the future. Above all, always remember how important it is for them to know that you love them.

> ➢ Don't assume they believe you don't care.
> ➢ Don't assume they want to believe this.
> ➢ Don't assume, even though they appear to at the moment, that this cannot change.
> ➢ Don't assume they are part of any attempts to discredit you.
> ➢ Remember they are half of you: what would they gain?

In normal circumstances, children will not choose to reject a parent completely.

Perhaps the following thoughts might persuade parents that indeed they do have much to lose in the long run, if they will not let their children go, or do not realise the damage they are doing.

Children, free to love both parents, not pressured to choose between them, will be less likely to resent either parent when they are mature enough to make sense of their family situation. Don't lie to your children, or deceive them. Don't encourage them to do the same. Lies are unsustainable. Sometimes years later, the missing pieces will be put together: *'That's not what I was told: is that true?'*

Finding out that one parent had lied about the motives of the other, had said they didn't care when in fact they cared a great deal, is inexcusable, and may result in rejection of the deceiving parent. It doesn't matter what the reasons may have been, or how behaviour was justified. Nothing can excuse the long-term damage to a child's self-image. *When it is suspected that they are being alienated against their 'other' parent, children undoubtedly need professional help without delay.*

This section ends with one father's suggestions for making the best of a difficult situation.

"Never miss out on contact. Never miss a phone call or be late for contact if you can help it. It is easy to be furious with the court for stopping you from writing more than one letter per week, and then six months later to not even keep up the one letter you are allowed. This is hard if the conditions are made awkward – e.g. only allowed to phone on Tuesdays between six p.m. and six-thirty p.m. – but you just have to do it.

Think of ways in which you can make the best of what little contact you have got, e.g. for young children, put stickers on the outside of the envelope so they look out for letters from you. Write your letters with coloured pens, or use a coloured printer to print different colours and big print. Include clipart and pictures from the internet. For older children, make sure you have a good website, so that they learn something about you from the pictures. There are lots of other ideas.

Be prepared to be a doormat for the sake of your children. Just bide your time, resist all provocation and don't complain. They'll see the way that you are being treated and that it isn't your fault. Keep up some kind of contact and as they get older and more independent they'll make sure that they get more. You'll miss out on their childhood, which is a great shame, but it can't be helped."

PART THREE: Basic Information

LEGAL FRAMEWORK

There are several key pieces of legislation concerned with divorce/separation and how they affect children and families. It would be helpful to familiarise yourself with these Acts, even if you are fortunate enough to sort out your arrangements relatively smoothly. The government departments that have responsibility for providing services for families produce a wide range of publications on all aspects of the law, policies and practices that may affect you. For the more detailed information you will need, start with the FNF website (and see Part Four).

It is essential to get to grips with the basic principles in the legislation. These will affect how decisions are made about your family. The following is a brief outline, not a statement of the law.

> ➢ All work from the fundamental principle that the welfare of children is *paramount*, i.e. must take first priority (but is not the *only* consideration).

> ➢ If the relationship between parents breaks down, it is considered best for children to have a continuing relationship with both parents and wider family.

> ➢ An integral part of most legislation is the belief that arrangements decided between the parents are preferable (the Child Support Act is an exception).

> ➢ All should be settled as quickly as possible, because delay is seen as harmful for children.

Court Orders concerning children

(Law and practices in Scotland, N Ireland and the Channel Islands may be different in some respects. Contact local branches for information.)

If parents cannot agree about arrangements after separation or divorce, a range of court orders can be applied for. The most common orders are made under the *Children Act 1989*. The court will not make an order unless they think it will be better for children if they do (known as the 'No Order' principle).

A **Residence Order** says with whom (but not usually where) the child should live. It can be made in favour of more than one person *(**Shared Residence Order** or SRO)*. The Children Act states that each parent retains parental responsibility after divorce and each may act independently of the other regardless of residence. SROs are usually made to stress the equality of both parents' role in children's lives. They do not necessarily define time to be spent in each home (although they may do so).

A **Contact Order** tells the person with day-to-day care of the child to allow contact between the child and the person named in the order. It can go into great detail about times, places and conditions. If conflict is anticipated, this is advisable and can remove any misunderstandings. If there is goodwill between parents, they can agree to vary the order.

The court is able to make orders which require specific actions (**Specific Issue Order**) to be taken or which prohibit certain steps (**Prohibited Steps Order**) being taken in respect of children. These orders are intended to safeguard the interests of the children where major issues of concern may arise and are not intended for trivial disputes.

The Children Act also covers **Parental Responsibility Orders** and 'public' law. Be aware of the difference between *private* and *public* family law. If you have to apply to court for anything concerned with divorce, separation, and arrangements for children, this is usually 'private' law. If there are reasons why the local authorities need to get involved, e.g. if there has to be an investigation by social services, because the children are thought to be at risk, this becomes public law.

There is a series of guides designed to help with applications to court (Part Four: No 24). You can download these (and the forms needed) from the internet or get them from your local civil (i.e. not criminal) court (see Types of courts p76). Making an application for an order is fairly straightforward if you get the information you need.

As with all other aspects, the helpfulness or otherwise of the court in providing these guides depends to a large extent on the individual you ask. Sadly, sometimes even the staff in the courts aren't up-to-date. Don't be put off. The guides are essential reading, explaining many of the terms used in the Children Act, the orders available and what they are for, and clearly show who can apply for them. They also answer some commonly-asked questions, so it's worth persevering.

Common practice

Although all is geared to *'the best interests of children'*, there are no hard and fast rules governing what this actually means. It therefore becomes a matter for individual interpretation. When making decisions, courts will also refer back to past court judgements (case law). In practice, delays are commonplace; applications are not necessarily simple. Some require many appearances in court. Where there are real differences, the process can stretch over many years, and still not resolve matters satisfactorily. Of greater concern is that current outcomes do not adequately reflect or encourage the principle of continuing contact with both parents and wider family, so clearly thought best for children.

Whatever your future involvement with the family justice system, if you eventually decide you may have to apply for a court order concerning your children, a working knowledge of the basic principles gives you a greater chance of understanding your options, and intelligently instructing your solicitor.

Legal aid

The cost of employing a lawyer to conduct your case is high, and the courts are under pressure to reduce the burden on the taxpayer – the cost of family breakdown to the public purse is estimated at over £5 billion a year.

Other than those on benefits, few fathers qualify for assistance with legal costs, and this has led to a growing number representing themselves in court – they simply have no choice. For those who qualify, the choice of solicitors is limited and the service can be rudimentary, but not everyone is confident enough to represent themselves and few would pass up the chance of assistance from a qualified professional. Legal aid may also be available for the costs of mediation. A common condition attached to legal aid is that any case should be commenced in the (lower) Family Proceedings Court (p76)

The provision of legal aid is another area undergoing substantial change, with the old Legal Aid Board being phased out. Its replacement, the Community Legal Service (Part Four: No 22) was launched in April 2000 and is intended to make it easier to resolve disputes by providing public access to legal information at libraries, law centres, Citizens Advice Bureaux, and via the internet.

UNDERSTANDING THE SYSTEM

"At the time of my divorce, I was at a complete loss what to do when I had hardly any contact with my children during the first three months. I found out about FNF by an opportune item on the radio."

If you decide or have no choice about legal action, the following is an overview of the 'family justice system', to familiarise you with some of the lessons learned by others, sometimes at great cost to their families.

Getting the right information can be the key to making positive decisions. The family justice system can be very confusing. You will need to find out as much as you can about how it operates, the language used, and the professionals you may meet, as early as possible. *If you need information, don't be afraid or embarrassed to ask for it.* If the first person you speak to isn't helpful, ask someone else. If you are not sure what's happening, who people are, find out. It's your family, although sometimes it may seem that everybody else appears to know more about it than you do! Because they work in the court situation day in, day out, they may forget that not everyone is as 'at home' as they are. They also forget that jargon they use all the time may be like a foreign language to you. You need to make sense of it: ask for an explanation if you don't understand.

The following is only a brief introduction to some of the services that may become involved with your family as you divorce or separate from your partner. FNF produces comprehensive guides to some of these services (details in Part Four). Also note that there will be differences in Scotland and N Ireland. Contact local branches in those areas.

A reflection of membership feedback:

"Exhaust all the other options before going to court. Find a more constructive forum to allow the children's needs to be given priority."

"Once an application to the court has been made, you must wholeheartedly see it through, unless better alternatives present themselves. Too many fathers, especially the best and most decent among them, give up because it seems too painful for all concerned. This short-term reduction in stress can mean a long-term loss for children."

The Family Court

Many families fail to reach agreement, for all kinds of reasons. If after exploring all other ways to sort out arrangements you still cannot agree, you may have to take legal action. To repeat earlier advice, it is crucial that you act swiftly if contact between your children and yourself is stopped or is resisted, because delay can damage both your relationship with them, and your chances of reinstating contact.

> If you do decide to apply for an order, you should still continue 'parallel' attempts to reach agreement with the other parent. Always remember that once the court or other professionals become involved, they have extensive powers and discretion to make decisions for your family.

Be aware that going to court is not straightforward. There are no easy solutions when parents cannot agree. Don't assume that the court is any better at finding 'the answer' to your problems. Don't assume that they will be interested in being 'fair' to you or the other parent.

All that can happen is that everything presented to the court should be considered in relation to how it affects your children. A decision will then be made based on what is thought to be the best course of action for children (note: not the parents). Be prepared to prove you put your children's interests first. If you feel they would benefit from more contact, ask for regular reviews. Draw up a plan for contact increasing over time. This shows you have thought things through.

You may find that the whole court experience is very different from what you expect, and the outcome not what you had hoped for.

"I represented myself in my own case, and am a frequent McKenzie (p79) for others and I can say that the only predictable thing is that the outcome is unpredictable!"

75

It is common to have to make more than one application. Don't expect the court to settle everything finally: situations and people change. Court orders may define some things, but cannot cover everything. You may need to make further applications at any time.

Types of courts

It makes life more confusing to discover that there are different types and levels of courts to deal with family matters as follows:

- ☞ **High Court** (London): the case is likely to be heard by more senior and experienced judges.
- ☞ **County Courts:** where a district or circuit judge will hear the case.
- ☞ **Family Proceedings Courts:** usually consisting of a bench of lay magistrates guided by a court clerk.

Most applications can be made in either of the last two courts, but certain applications (including the more 'difficult' cases) are made direct to the High Court. The case will usually be heard at the court nearest to the child's home. Family cases in England and Wales are heard 'in private' with the press and public excluded, so you will not be able to observe other cases. The **Appeal Court** (London) deals with appeals against earlier court rulings.

Choosing a solicitor

Most people think that they must go to a solicitor when faced with decisions about separating from their partner. However, this could be a big and expensive mistake. If you find you cannot manage without professional help, *be warned, not all solicitors can 'do your divorce' for you.* You will need one that specialises in family law.

Some legal practices are affiliated to the Solicitors Family Law Association (SFLA), whose Code of Conduct recommends handling family cases in a manner which minimises conflict, especially for children. This does not guarantee good service or ensure that the outcome for your family will be any better. Many FNF members lose confidence in solicitors, even well-known expensive ones. Lawyers will tell you 'A fool is his own lawyer', but some members will tell you quite the opposite (Representing yourself p78). As with all things, the quality and type of service you will pay for varies enormously, and many are dissatisfied with their lawyers. Much depends on the individual who eventually takes on your case. It takes talent and years of experience to be a good family lawyer. They do exist but finding the right one to represent you may not be straightforward. Recommendations, even by other FNF members may not be enough: what suits one family may be inappropriate for another.

It is a bit of a minefield, and the unwary should read the FNF guide to choosing solicitors. Even if desperate for legal advice, always find out as much as you can before making a decision.

More advice from members:

"You must instruct legal representatives to act as you want them to. You know the case better than they do. Don't let them sell you short. They may try to persuade you that the best you can hope for is the 'normal' outcome, i.e. one 'resident' parent. Accept this and you become the 'visiting' parent. There are other arrangements that enable children to benefit more easily from the support of both parents."

"Shared parenting should be the norm, and enforced, so that children can gain love and support from both parents and the wider family."

It must be borne in mind that there may be greater awareness of alternative outcomes, but courts change slowly, and are very conservative. Professional advice may be based on experience of what is a likely outcome (i.e. children will live with one parent, usually the mother). Anyone substantially disagreeing with 'the experts' may be perceived as 'being unreasonable', may even end up with getting less that the 'norm'. It is a dilemma: only you can decide what seems to be the best way forward for you and your family. FNF's statement on shared parenting 'The Presumption of Shared Residence' is essential reading (FNF booklet: see Part Four).

Beware of legal costs

It is quite easy to rack up rapidly a £20,000 bill: tens of thousands of pounds are not uncommon, even where things are fairly straightforward. Disputes about financial matters are usually the most expensive. Many solicitors are less than candid about the running costs of the case. Remember that they charge for time taken to do anything connected with your case. That includes answering telephone calls, photocopying etc., as well as writing letters on your behalf, giving advice or acting for you in court. It also includes the whole conversation with you, so cut through the social niceties as quickly as possible and get down to business. It's essential to establish what rate per hour will be charged: it shows you will be keeping an eye on costs.

> ➤ Take a list of all addresses, and anything else that otherwise might have to be recorded at the appointment.
> ➤ Before you go, make a list of what you want to deal with and take it with you.
> ➤ Ask advice on the best way to proceed, based on the list.
> ➤ Leave as soon as you have got the advice you needed, and have instructed accordingly.
> ➤ Make sure you are given draft copies of any letters so you can approve them *before* they are sent.
> ➤ Remember that it's *your* case. Ask for copies of all paperwork and organise in a file. It's surprising how much can be generated.

If you apply for legal aid, your solicitor will be unlikely to do anything more than offer a brief consultation (and perhaps write a letter) until your entitlement is decided, and this can cause delay. Ask how long it will take and check progress if necessary. If you do qualify you should be aware that you may still have to pay part of the costs of the case.

Don't be embarrassed to follow this advice: others have learned the hard way that legal costs can be ruinous, for them and for their families. Most important of all, if you do employ a solicitor, remember that they charge a great deal for their time and services, *whatever the outcome of your case.*

Representing yourself

FNF members often choose to represent themselves in court. They may not be eligible for legal aid, but still cannot afford the huge legal costs that can mount up. Many do so because they believe it to be more effective, particularly if only one issue is involved.[3]

The procedures both inside and outside the courtroom will be unfamiliar. The legal jargon used also makes it difficult to follow what is happening. It makes sense to read up on what's likely to happen beforehand. Family proceedings are generally

---

3   Also read FNF leaflet 'Representing Yourself' – not everyone is suited to conducting their own case.

conducted with less formality than criminal cases. As long as you are polite and respectful (and do not waste time), you need not worry too much about procedural matters. A 'litigant-in-person' (LIP) is not expected to know the rules inside out, and the opposition's legal representative (if any) may even be under pressure to explain them to you.

FNF may be able to informally advise on how best to prepare a case and conduct yourself in court. For many years, members have acted as 'McKenzie friends' in the courtroom. It can be extremely helpful to have both practical and moral support from someone that 'knows the ropes' and more importantly, is there to help *you*, not simply to do a job.

Ask if another experienced FNF member will go with you to court. Until recently it was recognised that McKenzie friends could go into the court, and even 'in chambers' with you. Although not usually allowed to speak, they could take notes, keep you organised and perhaps as important, help you make sense of what has happened afterwards. It is easy to miss vital bits of information when nervous or uncertain. Unfortunately, recent rulings mean that it is now up to individual courts and judges to decide whether you will be allowed help. This varies across the country and cannot be predicted, as the following shows:

"At the door of the court the 'friend' who had provided the support, was refused entry by the usher, with the words 'we don't like McKenzie friends here – Mr (Smith) has no need to have a McKenzie friend'. It is impossible to predict, before appearing at the door of the court, whether such a person will be admitted."

All you can do is present yourself as reasonably as possible, and hope that whoever is hearing your case is sympathetic. Also, your McKenzie friend must be prepared for a waste of his time and effort. Usually, but not always, court staff are helpful to LIPs. Be warned that experienced lawyers are more familiar with the court procedures. They know what is likely to happen, what the choices might be. Some are not beyond trying to intimidate or bully you. If you cannot keep your cool (and remember emotional involvement can make this difficult), self-representation is probably not for you.

You must be properly prepared, and stick to the point. Your personal knowledge of the case is certain to be far greater than that of any lawyer. Therefore don't be put off by those who counsel all is doom and gloom, you have no chance of success, you'll be eaten by the barrister on the other 'side'. If you have thought through what you will say to convince the court you are more than willing and able to take responsibility for your child, and welcome being actively involved in his or her upbringing, what better argument is there? Your trump card is your honesty, decency and, above all, your love for your child. Your level of educational attainment or grasp of the law shouldn't come into it.

"A reasonable case presented reasonably has a good chance of success."

One last reminder: you may be so wrapped up in your own case that you completely forget to thank your McKenzie. It is also customary to pay his (or her) expenses, but they must not be paid a fee. *Note:* acting as a McKenzie for someone else is a good way to gain experience for your own application.

The Family Court Welfare Service (FCWS)

(England and Wales only)

The FCWS, along with other services that work within the family court, is being re-organised. Little is yet known about these changes, or how they will affect you and your family. FNF National Office will be able to advise on the latest developments. It is unlikely that you will have a clear idea about what the FCWS does.

> ***This is THE pivotal service that may become involved in decisions that are made for your family,***
> *especially if you cannot agree about arrangements for your children.*

It is crucial to get a grasp of who they are, what they do, and even more important, who they work for. After you make an application for a court order, a court welfare officer (CWO) will usually be appointed at the first court hearing. This is when the court will decide what should happen next. The CWO might be asked to write a welfare report for the court. The FCWS may also be involved in conciliation meetings (Mediation/conciliation p9).

Briefly, CWOs are charged with finding out whatever information the court may need to make decisions for your family. Their primary responsibility is to safeguard the interests of the children, and they will therefore be concerned with anything that may affect children. Depending on the circumstances, the court may ask them to investigate specific areas as diverse as accommodation for children, or allegations of domestic violence. They are supposed to focus on finding out what the children think or would like to happen, although this is limited by the children's age and maturity, and many other factors. Sometimes the officer does not see the children.

You should be given an information sheet about the FCWS, what the CWO will do, how to complain, etc. Make sure you read it: it's easy to overlook when snowed under with other paperwork. You can also get a copy of their practice guidelines, which give more detailed information (Part Four: No 27).

Practice varies depending on where you live. Each service has evolved according to local needs; e.g. a large urban service will be different to one serving a less densely populated rural area. It is also acknowledged that individual officers have different approaches to their work, and have wide discretion to work as they choose. All this makes it almost impossible to predict what to expect.

They may meet you and your ex-partner together and/or separately, with your children or not. They may visit your home, or ask you to their office. It is possible to ask the CWO how he or she will carry out the investigation, e.g. try to make sure that the children are seen with *both* parents. The FCWS has extensive powers to get information about you and your children from many sources, although they should inform you about this. You should also be kept informed about what the CWO is likely to recommend. The report itself may not always reflect what you are expecting, even if you have been kept up to date.

After conducting the investigation into your circumstances, the officer will then write the report for the court. The report usually contains recommendations for what they consider will be the best outcome for the children. The recommendations are usually followed, unless there are other reasons not to do so. You or your representative should be told when the report has been submitted to the court, and of your right to a copy. *Make sure you get this as early as possible.* If you are not satisfied with the accuracy of information or those opinions on which recommendations will be made, you will need time to try to get this changed. It is almost impossible to correct or query anything in the report once you get to the court. Making a complaint about how the investigation into your family case was conducted *after* an order has been made will not change the judgement.

The FCWS may also provide funding for mediation services outside the court and works closely with some contact centres. The work they do is therefore central to the family justice system.

You are advised to remember that the FCWS has considerable influence over much that happens within the court. The FNF guide to the FCWS is essential reading and also gives advice on how to conduct yourself when in contact with this service.
Failing to make a good impression could seriously affect the outcome for your family.

Using 'the system'

If you have to 'use the system' to find a solution for your family, be warned that there is no certainty of outcome, and many are deeply disappointed, even shocked by judgements made. Being told by a judge that you cannot see your own children is hard to swallow. But the decisions made in family proceedings are not necessarily final, and you may be successful on appeal. Failing that, it will normally be possible to try again later, especially if circumstances change.

As you seek help, bear in mind that those working in the system are just doing a job. They will only have a brief involvement with your family. When they have played their part, their interest is over. You and yours, however, will have to live with the outcome. Therefore don't expect too much, have a realistic idea about what can be done, whether solutions can be found. Get as much information as you can, and don't rely on miracles.

One of the biggest difficulties when trying to describe the 'system' is that there are so many variables to take into account. This makes the outcome or likely judgement unpredictable. It is widely recognised that views and approaches vary considerably even within each profession or service that you may need to work with.

If you are unfortunate enough to have to become involved in legal action, this means that the outcome of your case will be different depending on which people are involved on the case, which judge is in court on the day. Practices also vary depending on where your case is heard. It is therefore vital to get local feedback, before risking the future of your family on this lottery.

"Quite a number of the fathers who come to branch meetings have been so confused by the advice they have had, that they start to think not about what they actually want and instead are concerned only about what they might get. I find it helps them if they are simply asked, 'What do you actually want so far as the children are concerned?' When they formulate an answer to this, I have not heard one single father say anything that was absurd or unreasonable nor even completely unattainable. But by not having the answer clearly in their minds from the start they often become intimidated and wracked with guilt about possibly upsetting the children by asking for contact with them or for shared residence."

It is so easy to be 'outmanoeuvred' by the system. If you have the information, and know what you want, you have a better chance of achieving a positive outcome for your family.

SUMMARY: *FOR THE SAKE OF THE CHILDREN*

To sum up some of the main points raised by this guide, finding out what you need to know is just a start. Coming to terms with life after divorce or separation means making difficult choices, sometimes with limited options. No one is prepared for what happens when families split up. It can come as quite a shock if you find you are outside your children's lives. Continuing to be a responsible parent may not be as straightforward as you had imagined.

"Fathers are so important."

The positive contribution that fathers make to their children's lives is widely acknowledged. There are major initiatives to raise awareness of this valuable role, to encourage father-involvement, but you cannot expect the same support for your continuing involvement after your family splits up. In fact, what you may find is a complete reversal of attitudes. What happens if the other parent stops your children seeing you? If you then take legal action, your determination not to be cut out of the parenting picture may be misinterpreted.

"Why don't they just give up? If I was in a similar position I would."

To get this in perspective, would anyone advise a father *inside* a family to give up? It is quite astonishing how attitudes change once you have been put in second-parenting place. You will soon discover that this applies not only to attitudes within 'the system'. The other parent is the key to what happens next. Your continuing relationship with your children depends on their agreement and co-operation. If for whatever reason they do not want to encourage this relationship, it will not be easy for any of you.

Throughout the guide, you have been advised to act as positively and reasonably as you can, and to explore all available avenues to reach an amicable and workable solution yourselves. You have been encouraged to try to get some dialogue going, to try to explain what's happening to the children. However, this advice has often been followed by *'If this is not possible in your case...'*

The fathers (and mothers) who have fed into this project have direct experience of the reality of resisted contact. They are more than willing to enter into whatever negotiations may be necessary for their children. *The main stumbling block may be that no one else seems to want or need to talk to them.* They are effectively powerless if the other parent decides to exclude them.

"I'm his mother. I don't *have* to ask."

Undoubtedly after family breakdown, children are routinely losing contact with one parent, usually (but not always) their fathers. Can it really be best for them if they 'lose' or in the worst cases, actively reject half their family support network? There needs to be a radical re-think of what causes conflict after parents split up. At present,

giving one parent almost total control causes a power imbalance that is impossible to negotiate. A recent government consultation paper did seem to acknowledge this problem:

"Education programmes might also be introduced for couples who have split up, if one partner is frustrating the other in obtaining the contact with children which the courts have decided is in their children's best interests. In theory, courts can fine or even send to prison those who deliberately obstruct contact, but these remedies are frequently ineffective, if not counterproductive, and the courts use them only as a last resort. These programmes, in contrast, would be positive and constructive, showing how continuing contact with both parents is normally in a child's best interests.

(Supporting Families Consultation Paper 1998: Para 4.34).

Unfortunately, as at the date of this guide there has been no decision on these programmes, despite widespread recognition that *'implacable hostility'* is not being dealt with satisfactorily. It is time to concentrate on behaviour that damages children, ask what is preventing their continuing contact with this wider support network, rather than advising the non-abusing parent to 'back off'. Many countries are accepting the importance of more equal sharing of parental responsibility and care after family breakdown. Policies and practices concerned with children and family breakdown must reinforce the benefits of enabling children to know and be loved by their 'whole' family.

Until the necessary changes are made, you will hopefully be even more determined to share more fully in your children upbringing, and to *'draw the line in the sand'* when you feel that what is happening to your children is damaging, or what is asked of you or them cannot be justified.

"Never give up hope"

PART FOUR: Reference Section

FAMILIES NEED FATHERS

'Keeping Children and Parents in Contact since 1974.'
Reg Charity No 276899

FNF welcomes membership enquiries. Anyone concerned about children losing contact with their families is encouraged to become a member.

> **Address:** 134 Curtain Road, London EC2A 3AR
> **Telephone:** 020 7613 5060
> **E-mail:** fnf@fnf.org.uk

www.fnf.org.uk: The FNF website is the best starting point for internet information, with links to every site you could possibly need. You can also join FNF on-line.

FNF Publications (please send sae for current price list – discounts for FNF members):

Leaflets:	**Booklets:**
The Children Act 1989	The Presumption of Shared Residence
Parental Responsibility	The Family Court Welfare Service
Interim Contact	Schools and Parents
Change of Surname	International Child Abduction
Representing Yourself	Parental Alienation Syndrome
McKenzie Friends	Implacable Hostility
Contact Guidelines	
Locating Your Child	
Grandparents	
Effective Letter Writing	
Child Support Agency	
Family Mediation	
Choosing Solicitors	

OTHER SOURCES OF ADVICE OR INFORMATION

1 **AIRE Centre (Advice on Individual Rights in Europe):** 020 7924 0927 after two p.m. Can advise on the Human Rights Act and its impact on UK law.

2 **Association of Shared Parenting (ASP):** local contact numbers – 01793 851544 (Swindon), 01789 750891 (Stratford-upon-Avon) and 0121 4491716 (Birmingham).
www.sharedparenting.org.uk

3 **Citizens Advice Bureau (CAB):** Local phone numbers. A good starting-point for advice on a wide range of issues affecting families. Lots of related literature and 'where to go next' information. Can refer to other organisations, including local services.

4 **Child Abduction Unit (Lord Chancellor's Department):** 020 7911 7047.

5 **Children's Legal Centre:** Has a free and confidential legal advice and information service covering all aspects of law and policy affecting children and young people. Contactline: 01206 873935 (Colchester).

6 **Councils (local and county):** Provide a wide range of community services; may include toy libraries, play buses. Also information on nurseries, crèches, authorised child-minders.

7 *Family Law*: Monthly journal available at main libraries. Lots of relevant information and latest family 'cases'. Includes articles written by judges and lawyers. Also, on the internet, has a free Family Law Update service, containing summaries of cases, legislation and practice developments (start of 1997 onwards).
www.familylaw.co.uk

8 **Family Mediators Association:** 020 7881 9400.

9 **Family Policy Studies Centre (FPSC):** 020 7388 5900. The centre aims to provide up-to-date information about families in Britain and key research findings on family life and policies. Wide range of publications.
www.fpsc.org.uk

10 **Gingerbread:** Head office 020 7336 8183. Support and advice for lone parents, including fathers. Free advice line: 0800 018 4318. Each local branch is different,

so worth investigating. Can help with welfare advice, childcare issues.
www.gingerbread.org.uk

11 **Grandparents' Federation** *'Working with grandparents for children':* Helpline: 01279 444964 (Harlow). Produces a range of publications, and can also advise when there is social services involvement.

12 **Mothers Apart from Their Children (MATCH):** Deals with similar set of problems to FNF, but where the mother is the 'non-resident' parent.
www2.prestel.co.uk/theturn/match

13 **National Association of Child Contact Centres (NACCC):** 0115 948 4557 (Nottingham). Can provide literature that can help you come to terms with the aims of centres and reassure re outcomes for children. Also has literature to help children (Ben's Story, No 36 below).
www.naccc.org.uk

14 **National Association of Child Support Action (NACSA):** Advice and information on the CSA plus a Helpline. Also produces a reasonably priced 'Self-Help' pack. NACSA, PO Box 515, Tweedale, TF3 1WJ. Hotline: 01908 665646 (Milton Keynes)
www.nacsa.org

15 **National Family Mediation (NFM):** 020 7383 5993 or in local phone book.

16 **Parentline Plus:** Offers support to anyone looking after a child. Free, confidential helpline: 0808 800 2222.
www.parentlineplus.org

17 **Relate (National Office)**: 01788 573241 (Rugby).
www.relate.org

18 **Reunite (National Council for Abducted Children):** Advice line: 020 7375 3440.

19 **Shared Parenting Information Group (SPIG):** collates and promotes research information on shared parenting.
www.spig.clara.net

20 **UK College of Family Mediators**: 020 7391 9162.

GOVERNMENT DEPARTMENTS

(*INCLUDING USEFUL PUBLICATIONS*)

20 Links to selected general government sites including those below, plus brief description can be found at: **www.namss.org.uk/ukgov1.htm**

21 Child Support Agency (CSA): National Enquiry line 08457 133133 – answers basic questions, plus CSA literature can be ordered. Has a comprehensive website. **www.dss.gov.uk/csa**

22 The Community Legal Service (CLS): Designed to make it easier for the public to get legal help and advice (England & Wales only). Find out more via your local CAB (No 3 above), or access a wide range of legal information on the internet, via a powerful search engine. **www.justask.org.uk**

23 The 10 Downing Street website: includes interactive surveys, including a parenting forum. **www.number-10.gov.uk**

24 Court Service: Customer Services general enquiry line 020 7210 2266. All the Children Act application forms you are ever likely to need can now be downloaded from their website in pdf (Acrobat Reader) format. The forms should also be available from your local court, or the address below (BAPS, Further reading No 32). **www.courtservice.gov.uk/forms/fmenu_caf.htm**

25 Department for Education and Employment (DfEE): Publications Centre, 0845 60 222 60 (Sudbury). 'Schools, Parents and Parental Responsibility', June 2000, Ref DfEE 0092/2000 Guidelines to schools on providing information to parents, including a definition of 'parent'.

26 Department of Health (DoH): encompasses Social Services.

27 Home Office (HO): 'National Standards for Probation Service Family Court Welfare Work': best read *before* meeting the FCWS. Available from the Probation Service, London 020 7273 3469 **www.homeoffice.gov.uk**

28 Inland Revenue: Children's Tax Credit Helpline 0845 300 10 36

29 Lord Chancellor's Department (LCD): 020 7210 8500. Responsible for all aspects of the family justice system. Includes the Children and Family Courts Advisory Service (CAFCASS). Wide-ranging literature. Has a comprehensive website: lots of practical information, plus explains the thinking behind legislation, current priorities and research.
www.open.gov.uk/lcd

30 Cabinet Office: find out how to complain about a wide range of public services at: **www.cabinet-office.gov.uk/servicefirst/index/comp_ps.htm**

FURTHER READING

31 *Family Law*, Tony Wragg, Nutshell Series, 1998. Is inexpensive and easy to understand. Provides good concise information for the first-timer. Includes lots of case references.

32 *The Children Act and the Courts* (one for children, one for parents). Both versions may be available from local courts or from: BAPS, Health Publications Unit, Heywood Stores, Manchester Road, Heywood, Lancashire OL10 2PZ.

33 *An Introduction to the Children Act 1998*, HMSO.

34 *Family Law*, Textbook, Ed Malcolm Dodds & Consultant Ed, Lord Templeman (2nd edition 1999), Old Bailey Press.

35 *Absent Fathers?* Jonathan Bradshaw, Carol Stimson, Christine Skinner & Julie Williams, Routledge, 1999.

36 *Ben's Story: An Introduction to Contact Centres*, Linda Wyon, NACCC: 0115 948 4557 (a book written for children).

37 *The Child Support Handbook*, Alison Garnham & Emma Knights, Child Poverty Action Group, 1999.

38 *Dad's Place: A New Guide for Fathers After Divorce*, Jill Burrett, Ward Lock, 1996.

39 *Family Organisations and Associations in the UK: A Directory*: Edited by Jon Bernardes, a comprehensive list covering all aspects of family life plus short description of the aims of each organisation. Available from the Family Policy Studies Centre (No 9 above), 1995.

40 *Fathercare*, John Griffiths, Colt Books, 1997.

41 *Fatherneed: Why Father Care is as Essential as Mother Care for Your Child,* Kyle D Pruett, Free Press, 2000.

42 *Fatherhood Reclaimed,* Adrienne Burgess, Vermillion, 1998.

43 *Getting to Yes,* Roger Fisher (2nd expanded edition), Arrow Books, 1997.

44 *How to Make an Application in the Family Proceedings Court,* Paul Mallender & Jane Rayson, Blackstone Press, 1992.

45 *Lost Children: A Guide for Separating Parents,* Penny Cross, Velvet Glove Publishing, 2000: 01959 577079 (discount for FNF members).

46 *A Man's Place in the Home: Fathers and Families in the UK*, Charlie Lewis, Joseph Rowntree Foundation, 2000.

47 *National Family Mediation Guide to Separation and Divorce: The Complete Handbook for Managing a Fair and Amicable Divorce*, Thelma Fisher, Vermillion, 1997.

48 *Outrageous Fortune,* Terence Frisby, First Thing Publications, 1998.

49 *Parenting Threads: Caring for Children When Couples Part,* Erica De'Ath, National Stepfamily Association, 1992.

50 *Unreasonable Behaviour*, Jim Parton, Simon & Schuster, 1997 (available from FNF National Office, discount to FNF members).

51 *Why Are My Parents Separating?* Diane Louise Jordan, from the 'Coping With Growing' Audio Series, Backbone Productions Ltd, 2000, **www.copingwithgrowing.com**

AND FINALLY

If you have found this book useful, help us to make future editions even better. Attitudes and practices in legal and social policy are rapidly changing. Your experiences can help others – make sure we hear about them. Write or e-mail to:

The Editor
For the Sake of the Children
FNF National Office
134 Curtain Road, London EC2A 3AR
E-mail: fnf@fnf.org.uk

Keeping Children and Parents in Contact since 1974

Index

Notes

Notes

Notes

Notes

Notes